"At 9:00 p.m. last night, my book hit #1. Thank you for your supreme guidance and expertise in starting this book."

— Cristina DiGiacomo, M.S.
Author of *Wise Up! At Work*, C-Suite Network Advisor

"I heard those magic words: 'We're here to help you succeed.' Then Donna and the team delivered. Her process is straightforward, and she was with us to make it happen. We have content for a second book because we've been recording and broadcasting the *Exitology* show. It's for marketing and to open doors to new listeners and colleagues—as we build our national platform like never before."

— Jason "Wally" Waldron,
Exitology: Unlock Your Profits, Unlock Your Potential

"If you want to be a professional podcaster and get your book written, look no further than Donna, Ben, and IBGR. They share a wealth of experience in a way that is easy to understand and use. Their enthusiasm is infectious, and they are a joy to work with. I've gained so much insight that's helping me reach more people with my message."

— Jeremy Gray, BusinessInAsia.Org

"I am fortunate to have gained a six-figure client before my book was done, thanks to Ben Gioia's coaching and mentorship around my business. Just need to finish the book now!"

— G. M., Speaker, Author, CEO

"Donna, Bill, and IBGR are the "pied pipers" of global business radio that transform businesses and lives."

— Mike King, The Voice of RVA Business on
ESPN Richmond Radio, CW Richmond TV, IBGR

"I cannot imagine podcasting without Donna and the IBGR Network! There's an amazing process for setting up a whole season of podcasts. They guided me with templates, examples, tools, and feedback to help me create a professional show syndicated to all major podcast platforms. Not to mention my global radio show that reached 183 countries! I accomplished much more than I thought was possible for my podcast. Thank you."

— Wayne Carroll, Patent Attorney,
Inspired Idea Solutions, LLC

"Donna Kunde has been our guide as we have created our show, *Stories Matter: Helping Leaders Transform Lives*, on The International Business Growth Radio Network. She showed us how to leverage our content into podcast episodes. She explained the process in a manner that allowed us to focus on what was important at the moment, keeping us from getting mired in the weeds. She has unveiled new information at a steady, digestible pace, allowing us to reap the reward of our investment in the network. She and Bill Eastman have enabled us to shine."

— Gayle Turner, President, The Storytellers Channel, Inc.

"What a fantastic experience this has been. Hosting my show and interviewing entrepreneurs from around the African continent has been a life changer for me, and it's a massive thanks to Donna and Bill for their endless patience and kindness—seeing the value of the show and the guidance that has gone with it. The IBGR Network is a valuable platform for entrepreneurs worldwide, particularly our beautiful continent—Africa. Let's grow this network and help more people to grow their businesses! Thanks so much for everything!"

– Glenda Thompson
Chartered Public Relations Consultant (PRISA),
GetUNoticed.co.za

"If I hadn't joined Ben's group, my book would still be on my computer. It would still be there, and I would still wonder if it was okay, if it was the right time, if I could do it, and if I had something to say. Being a part of Ben's program and working with Ben and Chris allowed me to do it. And I'm really, really proud of it! And can I share one thing? I'm talking at Google next month! Somebody read my book at Google! And they're going to pay me! And so that's like—brain exploding! Thank you, Ben."

– Annemarie Shrouder
Author: *Being Brown In A Black and White World,*
Consultant: Diversity, Inclusion, and Belonging

The Influencers Formula

The Simple Way To Create a Global,
Thought Leadership Masterpiece with a
Podcast, Book, or TV Talk Show

Ben Gioia
and
Donna Kunde

Foreword

Creating a masterpiece requires patience, mostly with yourself. I write this because recently, I crossed a personal desert into single parenthood. After a nine-year hiatus from the corporate world, I was in a brand-new arena where the stakes were suddenly higher, constant, and almost deafening. Seeking relief, I dove headlong into personal development. I learned about energy and manifestation, took yoga classes, and followed every thread offering "free" help online.

Oddly, this created more noise and confusion until I found myself awake at 4:00 a.m. wondering, *Who would take my distress call?* I felt the sharp edge of crisis when a thought came from the darkness all at once.

Ask yourself.

I pushed aside fear and stepped onto my yoga mat with a brand-new focus, wondering what my body (and beyond) would tell me. It was the beginning of a new relationship with myself as storyteller.

It's not a new idea, but it opened the understanding that *I was the one* I had been waiting for. Then, almost right away, two mentors appeared (Ben Gioia and later, Donna Kunde).

When anyone offers a simple solution, I typically balk because (most of the time) there's no such thing. But Donna and Ben break the mold. Few of us do it, whether creating a podcast or writing a book. And even fewer can successfully leverage their creation into income, freedom, and a shift in the global paradigm—even if it's just in a tiny corner of the world.

Donna and Ben's superpowers appeal to my core values. Vulnerability is strength. Authenticity opens hearts. And business excellence (with integrity) helps make society better for everyone.

And for all of us, there are struggles and some dark nights of the soul.

But that doesn't matter. What does matter is deciding your voice matters.

So, make that decision.

Your voice matters.

My voice matters. And I'm grateful to share my voice as a podcaster, an author, and a TV host.

If you're reading or listening to this book, you are already on the path. Congratulations, game changer!

People in the world are waiting specifically for you—right now.

I'd like to share some advice from someone who goes off track and gets lost—often on purpose. Trust the way of the book in your hands. Donna and Ben offer a shared voice that will change your business and life if you stay open to that possibility. I have yet to meet more gifted and unpretentious guides. Their reminders to trust the process—and yourself—are profound and compelling.

Oh! And if you're like me, you'll want to know, do, understand, and implement everything at once—yesterday. However, what lies in the following pages is practical, actionable, strategic, multi-million-dollar guidance from two masters.

So, smile (Ben often reminds me) because, no matter what, you're in for a treat.

Remember, your voice matters. Your story matters.

YOU MATTER.

I welcome you to this grand adventure with so much love and gratitude!

— Anna Devere, Author of *Seeing Like a Storyteller,* Co-Host of Discover Your Potential, TV/Radio/Podcast Host, Singer/Songwriter, Speaker, and President of Q1 Network

Table of Contents

- If you're a leader, speaker, coach, consultant, solopreneur, entrepreneur, or small business owner, this book is for you. Debunk the biggest myths, mistakes, and misperceptions so you can skip the bad decisions that cost most people a dozen years and a couple of million dollars (at least).

- It's easier than ever to create a global, thought leadership masterpiece and amplify your message and elevate your business. And that's extra good news because the world needs leaders like you, now more than ever.

- How would you like to be attracting revenue and making an impact even before your podcast or book is done? Discover ROI RIGHT NOW and let's toast to your success!

Our Warmest Welcome to You

Hi, it's Donna and Ben,

People often ask us, *Donna and Ben, how do I stand out so I can make a bigger impact with my message—and have the freedom and lifestyle I want?*

Our answer starts with these words from our wise friend Abe:

> "Give me six hours to chop down a tree, and I will spend the first four sharpening the axe."
>
> – Abraham Lincoln, 16th US President

In the pages of this book, you'll be sharpening your axe and chopping away.

You're about to discover the same tools, techniques, strategies, and perspectives we use to make success happen and make a bigger impact. Not to mention the ones we use to help our clients attract five-figure speaking gigs, six-figure consulting, stellar partnerships, and so much more.

We're grateful to help you make the good choices that bring high-ticket clients and profitable opportunities—instead of losing dozens of years and millions of dollars.

Imagine this: No more waiting around for that final chapter or last episode. Because you're on the fast track to more influence, income, and impact... even before you're finished!

Imagine this: You have a top-quality podcast or book (or both)—bringing you leads, clients, and opportunities—and instantly positioning you as a unique expert or authority.

Imagine this: You never have to worry about competing for business. Enjoy financial-, time-, and creative freedoms so you can share your message and make a difference!

We invite you to chat with us soon so we can say hi and you can get clear on your next best steps.

Visit www.DonnaAndBen.com today to see what's possible!

In the meantime, thanks for being here and reading these words. May they support your happiness, health, success, and impact!

Cheers,
Donna and Ben

Part 1

Why This Book, Where to Start, Why Now, and Who It's For

If you're a leader, speaker, coach, consultant, solopreneur, entrepreneur, or small business owner, this book is for you. Debunk the biggest myths, mistakes, and misperceptions so you can skip the bad decisions that cost most people a dozen years and a couple of million dollars (at least).

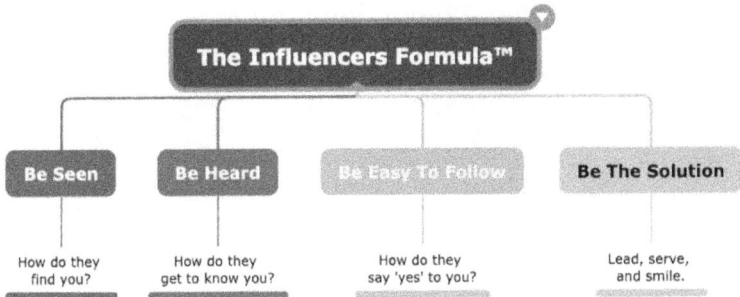

The Influencers Formula™

Be Seen	Be Heard	Be Easy To Follow	Be The Solution
How do they find you?	How do they get to know you?	How do they say 'yes' to you?	Lead, serve, and smile.

Where to Start

Right here! You're in the right place, especially if you want more leads and clients so you can amplify your voice, reach, and impact.

And if it's time to launch, rebrand, and amplify your business, then welcome. We love that you'll discover a whole lot of goodness that you can put into practice.

Because knowledge without action is, at best, a fleeting pleasure and fantastic distraction. We'll show you how to be a global thought leader with a message, product, or service that transforms businesses and lives.

Creating your podcast or getting your book done is a great way to make this happen. And you can use either (or both) to attract more clients and opportunities, even while you're writing or recording.

Your podcast or book gives you instant authority and credibility as your readers and listeners begin to know, like, and trust you. (That's why they will choose you over the hundreds, if not thousands, of other choices out there.)

Thanks for being here, and we invite you to keep reading.

Because in the following pages, you'll know how to avoid and transform common roadblocks like impostor syndrome, procrastination, and overwhelm that keep most people stuck.

So we ask that you stay fully present and open. Keep breathing, smiling, and playing at your full power.

The more you smile, the better your life will be. You smile when you're happy. And science proves that we can get happier when we smile.

When you smile, it's easier to relax and let things go. This is key for getting your book or podcast done.

To get a book manuscript done in just five to thirteen weeks, I (Ben) always remind my authors: *A light mind—is the right mind—to write.*

Same goes for your podcast or TV talk show.

Smiling (and letting yourself relax) is one of the most effective ways to keep from getting derailed by all the "stuff" that stops most people:

> "Stuff" like getting started, how to publish (without having to sell your children), fear, doubt, imposter syndrome, 'writer's block,' where to start, shame, 'lack' of discipline, fear or rejection, fear of being on camera, loss of the tribe, over-thinking, self-sabotage, self-judgment, what to actually write, where to start, lack of self-worth, monkey mind, overwhelm, confusion, your inner critic, and/or that feeling of, *It's so much bigger than me!*

So smile.

Because we're inviting you to stretch your comfort zone. Just 10 percent. This is a safe space, and we invite you into what's possible for yourself, your business, and the people you serve.

You'll have the keys to doing your podcast, book, or TV talk show the right way.

Because making the choices that bring high-ticket clients and profitable opportunities is infinitely better than losing a dozen years and a few million dollars (at least).

- Did you know that your book (or your podcast) can be turned into at least 25 more pieces of content (some instantly, some with a few minor tweaks of the dial)?
- Did you know you can get 5 percent of a 25,000-word book done in just seven minutes... without AI?
- Did you know that you can start marketing—and generating revenue—before your book or podcast is done?

That means that you don't have to wait to be serving your people right away.

This book is an ongoing invitation. To choose the simplest ways to get the right things done in your business so you can live more of your life.

Pretty cool, hey?

So keep smiling.

As you read (or listen), notice when things come up. Keep smiling and letting go of the stories that might keep you stuck. Take 100 percent responsibility for your experience.

Because there are a lot of myths and misconceptions about podcasts, books, and TV talk shows.

These myths and misconceptions become misunderstandings and false beliefs that keep some folks stuck while keeping others from starting.

So, remember:

1. Thanks to your book, podcast, or TV talk show, you can easily get one high-ticket client (whether that means $5,000, $50,000, or $500,000)
2. *But be careful* because it's easy to make mistakes that can easily cost you ten years and two million dollars or more

3. So keep reading and taking notes. Because when you know the truth(s)—and have the tools—you'll have no worries

Why this Book is Right on Time

This is a critical time in our history, planet, and for all living things. There's so much suffering, and the world needs more leaders. Whether in families, neighborhoods, businesses, governments, or our global community, there's never been a greater need for leaders.

That means that there's never been a greater opportunity for you.

(Wait, what?)

You read that right.

There's never been a greater opportunity for you to help transform the world—and your own business and life—by sharing your story. Especially on your podcast, in your book, or on your TV talk show.

In times of uncertainty (right now), there are people who need you to stand up and stand out. They're waiting specifically for you.

What's the answer? In a nutshell, it's to be seen, be heard, be easy to follow, and be the solution. That's The Influencers Formula™, and you'll hear more about this later.

Then it's so much easier for your audience, customers, collaborators, and clients to:

1. Find you and connect with you
2. Sign up for your list

3. Follow you and share on social media
4. Purchase your products
5. Invest in your services
6. Bring you more word-of-mouth referrals
7. Give you the opportunity to lead them or help them so they create more influence and impact with their business, their workplace, and their life

But people need to know what you're talking about, whether it's:

1. Face-to-face, on the phone, recording a video, creating a product, running a virtual meeting, or speaking to an audience
2. Giving a speech, webinar, or training (so you can inspire more people, give them a new perspective, and show them powerful and positive next steps on the road to their success)
3. On your website (so the right people will be engaged, read your content, and join your list)
4. In your emails (so people will open, read, and click to take action)
5. On LinkedIn (so the opportunities and partnerships you want will come your way)
6. During your discovery calls or on your sales page (so you can rocket your influence, get more clients or customers, and make a bigger impact)

Great communication is critical for great leadership

As we said before, you're a leader whether you're an executive, entrepreneur, solopreneur speaker, small business owner, coach, trainer, consultant, or other visionary committed to making a positive change in the world. You are shaping the future and your reality. You're bringing your vision, story, message, idea, product, or service to the world.

1. Begin with empathy. Get to know your audience and speak to them in their language about what's most important to them.
2. Ask people to share their stories with you. Ask questions. Ask more questions. Go deep.
3. Share your story so folks can get to know, like, and trust you... while positioning you as the leader, expert, and/or thought leader you truly are.

When you take these three steps, the magic happens. You understand them. They understand you, and you have everything you need for an authentic human connection that sets the stage for real transformation.

Who this Book is For

*T*he *Influencers Formula* is for you, but only if you want a roadmap for instant expertise and thought leadership with a podcast, book, or TV talk show you're proud of.

It's also for:

- People who want to amplify their income, influence, and impact
- The 87 percent of folks who are not (yet) sustainably making six or seven figures
- People who understand the power of starting to do marketing, partnering, and revenue generation—long before their podcast or book is published (or even finished)!
- Folks who don't want to die with their story inside
- You, if you want to live your life without regrets

Regrets suck.

And we're so fortunate! Think about it for just a moment. We have more power, choice, and flexibility in our businesses than ever before.

Like a client, Annemarie, who wrote her book and was then invited to speak at Google—thanks to her book!

To that end, we invite you to absorb the wisdom of Brian Chesky, co-founder of Airbnb. Because he invites us to create something loved by one hundred people instead of something that a million folks only kind of like. In Donna and Ben's language, find your best people and serve the heck out of them.

Because now is your time.

How To Use This Book

Wat you'll find in the following pages will help you make a bigger impact in the world with a podcast, book, or TV talk show.

You're about to discover concepts, perspectives, and strategies that you can use right away. They're presented clearly, simply, and directly so you know exactly how to use them.

We call it The Influencers Formula™ Roadmap, and we'll continue to lay it out for you in the pages of this book.

If you notice that you're rushing, slow down. Relax your head, relax your face, and smile.

Breathe.

This isn't like any other book you've read (or listened to) because it's saturated with proven takeaways that are aligned with timeless, transformational wisdom.

Here's just some of what to expect.

- In Part 1, we're debunking the biggest myths, mistakes, and misperceptions about podcasts and books. You'll also see how to avoid the bad decisions that cost people a dozen years and a couple of million dollars (at least).
- In Part 2, you'll see how easy it is to create a global, thought leadership masterpiece so you can amplify your message and elevate your business.
- In Part 3, we'll open the doors so you can focus on attracting revenue and partners right out of the gate (ROI right away).

- In Part 4, you'll discover more about making yes easy, referral triggers, and the many voices of story. Plus, what you need to know about meditation, imagination, and the power of your subconscious for bringing your message to the world.
- In Part 5, it's an unexpected combination of false beliefs, forgiveness, and leadership lessons from Nelson Mandela.
- In Part 6, we dig into business podcasting made easy, writing your book faster than the average bear, and how to skip paying your publisher an extra $180,000. You'll also discover the million-dollar timeline, how to choose your best stories, and how to make sure your podcast (or book) will work.

Our intention is that you take what you learn—plus the wisdom you cultivate and the insights you experience—and create the influence, income, and impact you want. We wish you every possible success and more!

Because yes, you can do cool things like a client, Monica who got a five-figure speaking gig before her book was even published!

Now, we invite you to take a few moments to be present to get the most out of what's inside. Shut the door, put your phone on airplane mode, and get comfy.

Have a notebook handy, get some sticky notes, scribble in the margins, dictate your thoughts into your phone, and capture your discoveries.

Take a few deep, nourishing breaths, and smile.

Here we go!

Part 2

The Magic of Podcasts, Books, and Radio

It's easier than ever to create a global, thought leadership masterpiece and amplify your message and elevate your business. And that's extra good news because the world needs leaders like you, now more than ever.

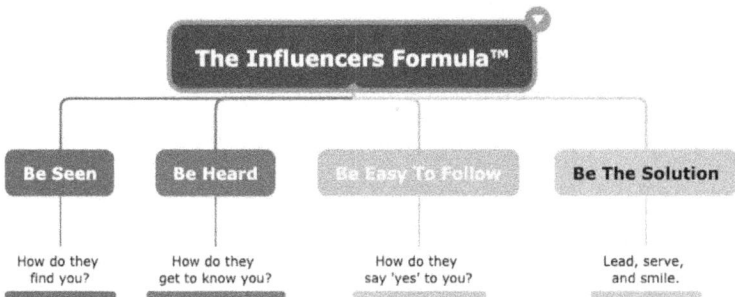

The Influencers Formula™

| Be Seen | Be Heard | Be Easy To Follow | Be The Solution |
| How do they find you? | How do they get to know you? | How do they say 'yes' to you? | Lead, serve, and smile. |

The Magic of Podcasts and Books

There's a simple reason for this book: to help you create a global, thought leadership masterpiece that elevates business and changes lives. (Although we'll look most closely at podcasts and books, we'll also introduce you to TV talk shows if you haven't discovered them yet.)

We promise you this: If you read this book and put what we're sharing into action, you will know how to make an impact as a highly paid expert, authority, or thought leader with your podcast, book, or TV talk show.

Like a client, Wally, who already has content for a second book because of his podcast. He's using it for marketing, attracting more clients, colleagues, and building a platform, fast.

Are you tired of waiting for your podcast or book to be finished before you can start making connections and sealing those lucrative deals?

We hear you! Thanks to this book, you get to do things right.

So, let's start with an array of great news about books, podcasts, and TV talk shows.

- People love books (whether reading or listening). That means a well-executed book is always brilliant for your business. (Your book is one of the best tools for getting clients, even before it's published or finished.)

- There are 464.7 million podcast listeners globally as of 2023.
- The US has the most listeners worldwide and is predicted to have over 100 million in 2023.
- *Professional* self-publishing has opened the doors for people who want to amplify their income, influence, and impact. You own your intellectual property (IP)—instead of the publisher—and get to benefit from print-on-demand (so you don't need to buy thousands of books that take up space in the garage).
- A third of the US listens to podcasts, with 41 percent monthly, 28 percent weekly, and 22 percent listening while driving or commuting. An average weekly listener hears eight episodes, and households with incomes of $100,000 to $150,000 are about 17 percent of monthly listeners.

– Podcast Data: Demand Sage

Don't forget the best part! With your podcast done (right), you've already created 80 percent of the content for your book. And with your book done (right), you've already created 80 percent of the content for your podcast!

It makes sense.

It drives revenue and impact.

It works.

And we've proved it.

How? Donna and Ben started by creating the Business Podcasting Made Easy podcast and global radio show (in just three months). Then, we leveraged that content to create a two-day live event and wrote this book you're reading or listening to (in just five months).

That means we have four assets in place—podcast, book, radio show, and live event)—that we created almost simultaneously. We followed The Influencers Formula™ Roadmap (which you'll learn about in the pages of this book), and we made it all happen in just eight months.

Did you catch that?

You don't have to create just one at a time. You can leverage your approach and collapse time instead!

Imagine the income, influence, and impact!

Podcasts and books bring leads, clients, partners, and opportunities. Every successful leader, consultant, coach, speaker, solopreneur, and small business owner has a podcast or book that works.

How about you?

Are you ready to let your light shine and let your voice be heard?

With this handy resource, you'll have everything you need... from idea to broadcast. Includes roadmap and audio training. Go here for Business Podcasting Made Easy: InfluencersFormula.com/resources.

A Better Lens for Leadership

M ore than at any other time in history, we need leaders who care about the good of the planet and our one human family. You're a leader, whether you call yourself that or not. You're a leader, whether you're helping one person or changing the lives of millions.

- You are shaping the future as well as your reality. You're bringing your ideas, vision, story, message, product, or service to the world.
- That means that it's critical to communicate with people in a way that educates and inspires them to take action.
- So, connect the dots from your vision to their goals and dreams. Don't assume they'll get it. Make the path clear.
- Do this with everyone your business touches.

Because there are myriad groups with a cornucopia of goals, challenges, fears, pains, hopes, desires, and dreams. So, keep connecting the dots. Leave that trail of breadcrumbs.

Like we've said before, you can't talk to all these people about the same things or use the same language.

1. Instead, begin with empathy. Get to know your audience and speak to them in their language about what's most important to them.
2. Ask people to share their stories with you. Ask questions. Ask more questions. Go deep.

3. Share your story so folks can get to know, like, and trust you... while positioning you as the leader, expert, and/or thought leader you truly are.

When you take these three steps, the magic happens.

You understand them. They understand you, and you have everything you need for an authentic human connection that sets the stage for real transformation.

Because if you think about it, leadership isn't about titles.

It's about caring for the people you serve while creating new realities in business, life, and the world.

Stories create new realities.

When you share your story, people will take an extra moment to read or hear your words. And when you listen to their stories, these people will realize you understand and care about them.

Because stories make ideas and concepts tangible while making books fun to read, podcasts fun to listen to, and speeches fun to hear. They help make the learning stick, so the things people discover become part of their muscle memory.

And what's super cool is that stories don't have to take hours. You can tell a story instantly with a gesture or with a smile. You can tell a story with an image, a handful of words, or a tweet. You can tell a story through video, email, or any medium that connects you to the people you serve.

This is important whether you're teaching, coaching, selling, serving, training, speaking, or leading. Because you're inspiring people. You're connecting the dots from your vision to their goals and dreams. You're educating and influencing people to make choices and take action that's good for them, good for you, and good for the world.

That's the power of story.

There isn't a social change, movement, or paradigm shift that's ever happened without stories.

When there are no stories, no one stays around to listen (or read or watch). But when you share your story, people can't stop listening to you.

Here Are 7 Things That Happen When You Use Story

1. Stories help people visit your website, join your list, schedule a consultation, invest in your products and services—and tell the world about what you offer—because it's changing their business and life for the better.
2. Stories will help make your business more profitable so you can make a bigger impact. People will remember you because of the stories you share.
3. You'll be influencing people to take action by appealing to reason *and* emotion.
4. When you discover and listen to someone's story, you create an ongoing opportunity for them to know, like, and trust you.
5. People are inspired to follow your lead because they understand your vision.
6. Although our world is chock full of different languages, cultures, and businesses, stories help us realize all the things that we have in common (one human family).
7. You'll impact more lives every single day!

Whether you're an executive, entrepreneur, speaker, small business owner, solopreneur, coach, trainer, consultant, or other visionary committed to making a positive change in the world, you are a leader.

And when you share your stories, people can't stop listening to you.

Our carefully crafted questions will help skip the mistakes that cost people five to ten years and millions of dollars. Go here and don't write your book until you're sure it will work: InfluencersFormula.com/resources.

The Magic of Radio

So many leaders, consultants, coaches, speakers, entrepreneurs, solopreneurs, and small business owners have the expertise. But they don't know how to launch, grow, and sustain a successful business. They also don't know how to create a radio show, podcast, book, or TV talk show the right way.

So before we go any further, let's go back in time just a few years.

In 2019, WNTW radio in Central Virginia implemented a new programming approach that led to profitability in just eight months. They focused on listener-based programming, local content, retro shows, and assisting business owners.

This success demonstrated the epic possibilities, especially when you create a global radio show that becomes a podcast—automatically.

Did you know?

- Radio is one of the most powerful mediums in the US, with a weekly reach of 82.5 percent among adults and over 15,445 radio stations
- After hearing a commercial on the radio, 46 percent of the listeners considered a purchase
- Almost 79 percent of daily audio listening is attributed to live radio, with 53.2 percent among 15 to 24-year-olds

— Source: Gitnux

Enter Donna Kunde and Bill Eastman, co-founders of The IBGR Network. International Business Growth Radio (IBGR) is an internet-only radio station with one big goal: to help people start and grow a successful and sustainable business, thereby eliminating global poverty through generational wealth. Because

- 57 percent of the world's workforce comes from 375,000,000 small business owners with 20 or fewer employees
- That's almost 2 billion people (and a huge contribution to the global GDP)
- Radio is a powerful tool that can help change the world. That's why Donna helps people create podcasts by simultaneously creating global radio shows that reach people in 184 countries!

Fear and Still Moving Forward

Fear is part of being human. Whether you're an entrepreneur, building a business, restructuring an organization, entering a new market, or needing more clients, there's likely some fear happening for you.

Fear feels yucky—whether it's dread in the heart, cold in the guts, or noise in the mind. Sometimes, fear shows up disguised as anger, impatience, procrastination, worry, anxiety, nervousness, lethargy, anger, grief, doubt, and more.

But nothing's wrong. And it's not your fault.

But it is your responsibility.

Although it can be difficult to believe, none of it is personal. Why? Because you didn't ask for the fear, anger, memory, or other unpleasant feeling (physical/emotional/mental/psychic) to happen.

Yet there it is.

So smile and relax and breathe. Repeat.

Don't push the unpleasant feelings away. Simply relax into them and just let them be. Don't take them personally. Don't get involved. Because that unpleasant feeling can keep you from moving forward.

So, for the sake of your happiness, your business, and the people you serve, don't let any of this stop you. Because you don't have to!

That's great news, and it's immediately empowering. (Because once you know the truth about something, you can't unknow it.)

So we invite you to practice not taking ANYTHING personally—again and again.

How?

When something comes up, relax your head, relax your face, smile, breathe, and repeat three times.

Then, get back to writing, recording, and changing lives!

Your Story and Your Voice Matter

We did a survey on LinkedIn and asked, *How old were you when you realized that you're an artist (however you define it)?*

Most people knew they were an artist/creative by age ten, with 70 percent of them knowing by the time they were 20 years old.

However, when asked, *How old were you when you truly knew, heard, or understood that your voice matters?*

A whopping 75 percent *didn't* know until they were over 21, with the majority *not* knowing until after 40!

We're here to tell you and remind you that your voice matters.

And yet creating the future you want—with your podcast, book, or TV talk show—can often feel overwhelming.

So replace overwhelming with exciting, you'll immediately enjoy a completely different experience. Because here's a beautiful opportunity to create more income and impact as you bring your dreams to life.

- The microphone will change your life
- Your book will change your life
- Your podcast will change your life

What Are You Discovering So Far?

_____

_____

_____

_____

_____

_____

_____

_____

_____

_____

_____

_____

_____

_____

_____

_____

_____

_____

_____

Introducing Donna and Ben

[from Donna] I'm Donna Kunde, the producer of over 14,000 podcasts and co-founder of IBGR.network. Thanks to my international business radio station (and network), I have the pleasure of amplifying over multiple experts in 14 countries, reaching listeners in over 184 countries, and delivering worldwide transformation every day.

Life is full of surprises. Not only am I amplifying voices and leaders through podcasts and radio, but I've also helped train 75,000 people (at the request of the Costa Rican government). I was named a "Top 50 Women Leader" of Virginia and played music for presidents, princes, generals, and ambassadors.

But it wasn't always like this.

I started my journey by sitting on the couch, waiting to die. (More on this later.)

And long before this, I was raised to be seen and not heard. This destructive programming and thought patterning led to multiple toxic relationships. Fast forward a few years, and I'm retiring from the United States Army. As I was sending my youngest off to college, I realized I had some money left on my GI Bill and time on my hands.

So, I took yet another coaching certification course. One assignment was to make a vision board. I began cutting up magazines and putting images on a page and noticed microphones at the top. And I said to myself (surprisingly), *I'm probably going to do a podcast.*

Long story short, I never, *ever* would have thought I would be the owner of a radio station and amplifying voices from around the globe to listeners in 184 countries!

What are the possibilities for you, your business, and your life? I invite you to imagine them, enjoy them, and then play with thinking even bigger!

[from Ben] I'm Ben Gioia ("joy-a"), a four-time best-selling author, podcast, and international radio show host. My teachings are used by over 80,000 leaders and game-changers around the world. I help folks write great books in as little as five weeks, enjoy five-figure speaking fees, and attract six-figure consulting. (That's before even publishing!). I've trained hundreds of millionaires and helped a Fortune 100 company create an empathy video game for 20,000 employees. With 39 years of writing and publishing adventures, I helped launch the world's largest magazine *(AARP)* and won a patient services award from The ALS Association for creating their first mindfulness program.

Similar to Donna, it wasn't always like this.

I've been writing and publishing since I was twelve years old. Throughout high school (yearbook) and into college (studying creative writing)…which led to a career in magazines (launching the world's largest at that time).

I used to do all sorts of drugs for entirely too long. But eventually, I found my way to meditation, which changed everything.

On the way, I faced death four times in seventy-two hours (in India) and trekked through the Himalayas for nine days with blisters on my feet. I discovered my purpose and understood the difference between pain (part of life) and suffering (optional). And how to eliminate suffering.

Then, just under ten years into my entrepreneurial adventure, I was asked to speak at Stanford (woo hoo!). I promised to show up with autographed copies of my brand-new book. (Although I hadn't written it yet!)

So, I wrote the book in three weeks, produced it in three more, and showed up with autographed copies for everyone in the audience. The rest, as they say, is history, which leads us to this book and our brand-new live event, The Podcast and Book Roadmap.

Thanks for being here!

Be Our Guest at Our Upcoming Live Event

THE PODCAST AND BOOK ROADMAP
The Simple Way to Create a Global,
Thought Leadership Masterpiece
(In Just 6–9 Months)

ATTENTION: Leaders, Consultants, Coaches, Speakers, Trainers, Solopreneurs, Entrepreneurs, and Small Business Owners

- Want more leads, clients, and impact?
- Is it time to launch, rebrand, and/or amplify your business?
- Ready for ROI, even before your podcast or book is finished?

BENEFITS and OUTCOMES:

1. Imagine this: No more waiting around for that final chapter or last episode. Because you're on the fast track to more influence, income, and impact... even before you're finished!
2. Imagine this: You have a top-quality podcast or book (or both)—bringing you leads, clients, and opportunities—and instantly positioning you as a unique expert or authority.

35

3. Imagine this: You never have to worry about competing for business. Enjoy financial-, time-, and creative freedoms so you can share your message and make a difference!

Join the next Podcast and Book Roadmap so you can be attracting revenue and making an impact before your podcast or book is done. To get your ticket (and save 50 percent), go to PodcastAndBook.com and enter coupon code PBRSPECIAL50 at checkout.

SNAPSHOT:
The Influencers Formula™ Roadmap

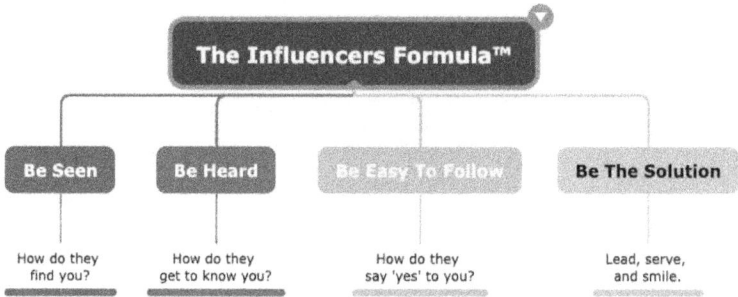

The Influencers Formula™

Be Seen	Be Heard	Be Easy To Follow	Be The Solution
How do they find you?	How do they get to know you?	How do they say 'yes' to you?	Lead, serve, and smile.

I f you stop and think about it, The Influencers Formula™ Roadmap (IFR) is a lot of high-impact goodness wrapped up in a little package:

- Be seen
- Be heard
- Be easy to follow
- Be the solution

That's it.

It's geared to help you make the good choices that bring high-ticket clients and profitable opportunities instead of the bad choices that lose you dozens of years and millions of dollars.

It's an empowering roadmap for stepping up and into global thought leadership with the right mindset and presence.

It works at the root by unblocking impostor syndrome, procrastination, and overwhelm, which keep most people stuck.

It's focused on helping you attract high-ticket revenue right out of the gate by developing the right relationships.

It's what a client, G.M., did to attract a six-figure consulting gig before their book was done!

It's the Antidote to What Doesn't Work

For the record, here are a few things that don't work.

1. Creating a podcast, book, or TV talk show without talking directly to your ideal clients about what you're creating
2. Not elevating, educating, and inspiring your readers, listeners, or viewers

3. Not articulating or magnifying the problem/pain/challenge to move the needle and help them take action
4. Too much information and not enough implementation, accountability, community, or support

So, we return to The Influencers Formula™ Roadmap. Be seen. Be heard. Be easy to follow. Be the solution.

And with that, sometimes people get nervous because of the 'M' word.

Marketing.

However that word makes you feel, turn the page for marketing like you've never seen before.

The Influencers Formula™ Roadmap (IFR) is a comprehensive path to instant expertise and thought leadership. Go here to get the keys to a top-quality podcast or book (or both): InfluencersFormula.com/resources.

Marketing With A Heart

There are years of negative perceptions about marketing and selling—everything from unpleasant to evil. But if you think about it, marketing and selling are service. Especially when you do them with the right intention and what you're offering will help people live happier, more productive, peaceful lives.

Old-school marketing is what you do *to* people—pressure, fear, manipulation, lies, false hope, sales tactics, and hard closes. (Think of the stereotypical used car salesman in a cheap suit or a late-night infomercial.)

Marketing With A Heart is what you do *for* people—educating, adding value, creating trust, developing relationships, and changing lives. It's a win-win-win.

Marketing With A Heart is a revolutionary philosophy and successful business strategy because it provides a personal approach to attracting money while making a difference.

Marketing is the language of service: expressed and shared.

Marketing is how you change lives with your message. When promoting, presenting, partnering, or producing, you must align people with your vision and inspire them to take action sooner or later.

- ***(Based on)*** PURPOSE. Purpose is the why that fuels your passion and your mission. It's the strategy for making your dreams into reality. It's how you balance your long-term vision with day-to-day action. Knowing what guides you from within helps you make the right decisions, even the hard ones. Knowing your purpose makes your work more fun and fulfilling and expresses who you are. You get more of the right things done faster and with much less stress. This supports your mission and ability to inspire, persuade, and transform people's lives. It's a win-win for everyone your business and life touches.

- *(Based on)* IMPACT and INCOME. While your message will change one life, your marketing can change thousands, if not millions, of lives when done correctly. It begins by getting to know your audience and speaking to them in their language about things they truly care about.

Marketing is how you communicate with and influence people in a way that inspires them to take action so they can be more successful, fulfilled, and have more fun. By communicating with authenticity and integrity, you can inspire people to make choices that benefit them and you.

Essentially, it's cultivating trust, building relationships, and inviting your audience to take action because you understand what they care about, speak to them in their language, and deliver value.

The extra good news is that you'll also attract the right people to form partnerships and strategic alliances so you can make an even greater positive impact in people's lives.

Because you're a visionary and leader, whether helping one person or changing the lives of millions, you're here for a reason, reading these words right now.

You have a message, product, or service you need to get out there. And you need to make the money that will support your mission, business, and lifestyle.

People need what you've got right now. There has never been a more pivotal time in history. As someone who wants to help people, you must know enough about marketing to effectively communicate with and influence your audience.

And not just any old marketing (like we said), but the right marketing. Because wherever you are right now is temporary and exactly where you are supposed to be. You've arrived at this moment to learn what you must learn so you can continue to become the person you need to be. And since you're reading this, I know you want to help people live happier, more productive, and more peaceful lives.

Us, too.

We're here to help you use the right language and deliver your message the right way to inspire, persuade, and transform lives for greater income, influence, and impact.

The Most Important Thing
In This Book

Yes, the whole book is important. (So, keep reading, gosh darn it!) And we invite you to remember this: When it comes down to it, there are a few things that motivate people:

1. The desire for happiness (and the avoidance of pain and suffering)
2. Wanting to overcome things like self-doubt, fear, worry, anxiety, or insecurity
3. The potential for greater meaning, purpose, and connection in a rapidly changing world in a vast and mysterious universe

How do you translate that into actionable, profitable, impactful intelligence for your podcast or book?

It's simple: Have conversations with your ideal clients about the book you're writing or the podcast you're creating so you can start attracting clients and partners right away.

When you do this, all sorts of good things happen. You know exactly what your people want and need—their reasons why and the language and words they're using. If you're clever (which you are), then this conversation also lays the groundwork for that person to become a client or a strategic partner.

Even before the podcast (or book) is finished.

It's ROI, right out of the gate.

Part 3

A Pyramid of Champagne Glasses

How would you like to be attracting revenue and making an impact even before your podcast or book is done? Discover ROI RIGHT NOW and let's toast to your success!

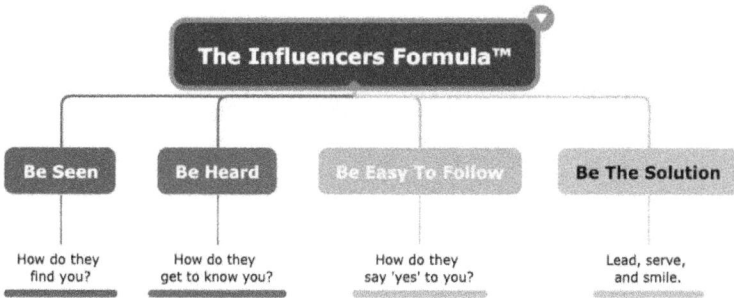

The Influencers Formula™

Be Seen	Be Heard	Be Easy To Follow	Be The Solution
How do they find you?	How do they get to know you?	How do they say 'yes' to you?	Lead, serve, and smile.

A Pyramid of
Champagne Glasses

Have you ever seen a champagne glass pyramid at a wedding (or seen it on video)? A pyramid with just six tiers will have 91 glasses! So, what's the best way to fill them all with champagne?

Simply pour the champagne into the top glass... and keep pouring!

Otherwise, it would be madness to pour 91 glasses when you can just pour into the top and let that one fill the others.

Now, imagine your podcast or book. That's the top glass of your pyramid. The champagne is your wisdom, expertise, and special sauce. And everything flows from there.

But wait, it gets even better.

You'll have 80 percent of your podcast done when you finish your book. You'll have 80 percent of your book done when you finish your podcast.

Then look at what you can create and leverage without much extra work:

1. A podcast or book (depending on whether you already have one or the other)
2. One-on-one coaching
3. A year's worth of content
4. Audiobook
5. A book series

6. A TV talk show
7. Consistent messaging
8. Consulting
9. A custom book for a client
10. An evergreen course
11. Expert positioning and instant credibility
12. Leads
13. Group coaching
14. Keynote speeches
15. A lead magnet
16. Licensing
17. A live course
18. Mentoring
19. A paid course
20. Part of package
21. Program delivery
22. Books to sell at events or offer them as part of your speaking fee
23. Speaking
24. Workshops
25. So much more!

How cool is that? Does this give you a few ideas?

We love the champagne glass pyramid. Can you see how this applies to your business?

Recycling, Repurposing, and Artificial Intelligence (AI)

We teach our clients leverage—how to create a ton of content by starting with their book or podcast, as well as using video, audio, and other assets they already have.

Recycling, repurposing, leveraging.

And we get a lot of questions from our authors and podcast hosts about using things like AI, ChatGPT, and more to make repurposing and leveraging much easier.

AI platforms can indeed turn your audio or video into ready-to-use content in a matter of minutes. Authors, podcasters, and creators of all types are using AI as a foundation for:

1. Pre-production tasks like podcast titles and show notes
2. Post-production that delivers transcripts, summaries, blog posts, newsletters, and social media posts

There are several great possibilities but be careful. Keep the following in mind when working with AI platforms:

- Don't give out personally identifiable information
- Ensure that confidential or sensitive data is appropriately anonymized or sanitized before using AI systems to minimize the risk of unintentional disclosure
- Don't give your intellectual property to a robot

- Stay informed about AI technology and security practices to proactively address emerging risks and implement necessary measures
- Consider the ethics of using AI so you can make informed choices about a tool that seems to have more and more of a "mind" of its own... it's your job to keep humanity in the technology
- Like anything else, understand your intentions and take responsibility for your actions

(More about AI later in this book.)

Part 4

Do You Know Who You're Talking To?

It's about making yes easy, referral triggers, and the many voices of story. Plus, meditation, imagination, and the power of your subconscious.

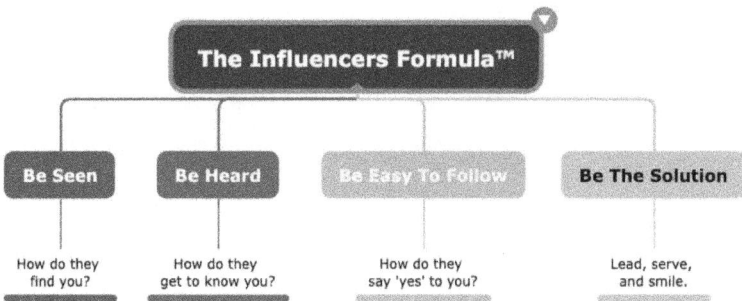

The Influencers Formula™

Be Seen	Be Heard	Be Easy To Follow	Be The Solution
How do they find you?	How do they get to know you?	How do they say 'yes' to you?	Lead, serve, and smile.

Who's Your Audience, Really?

S uppose you want to connect and develop a trusting relationship with your prospect, customer, client, colleague, or audience. In that case, you'll want to communicate in their language about the things that are the most important to them.

This means using the exact words and phrases they use when they describe their challenges, fears, frustrations, needs, experiences, hopes, goals, desires, and dreams.

Around the world, we speak different languages, practice different customs, and do different things. This is reality, and it occurs from country to country, business to business, culture to culture, generation to generation, situation to situation, and person to person.

That means it's critical to get clear on what's important to people—and how they talk about it—so you can create the most effective communication, rapport, and connection. To get started, do your research, talk to lots of people, and make sure you're as clear as possible with these three things:

- Key data (demographics) that can be measured include gender, age, income, marital status, etc. These are the "dry" (perhaps) and vitally important facts about your clients, customers, employees, team, market, or audience.
- Group trends (psychographics) such as behaviors, hobbies, spending habits, values/principles, product usage,

opinions, where they hang out online, interests, and lifestyle choices.

- Individual purpose and passion (sociographics) that goes deep, giving you an understanding of what motivates people: their personal needs, attitudes, fears, frustrations, goals, dreams, and what gives meaning to their lives.

When you do this, you will connect with people on an emotional and experiential level, which is what you want. Then, you have the right language for better marketing, tailored products and services, and leadership that creates real transformation.

Knowing as much of this information as possible will help you expand your sphere of influence as you discover other people connected to your prospect, client, customer, or audience. This allows you to serve a wider range of people, businesses, or organizations.

Here's how to uncover this information:

- Ask questions about people's biggest challenges
- Do your research
- Email a survey to your list
- Make phone calls
- Give a talk or live audio
- Offer a masterclass
- Start or participate in a LinkedIn, mastermind, or networking group that feels aligned

The more you know about your clients, customers, audience, colleagues, and market—from their day-to-day experiences to the deep, emotional, keep-them-up-at-night details—the more successful you will be.

1. You'll connect, communicate, and lead better
2. You'll reach more people with your ideas and message
3. You'll create a shared human connection and experience while getting people excited about who you are, what you're about, and how you will impact their business, life, or both
4. You'll create superior products and services that deliver exceptional value (based on what your people want and need because they've told you)
5. You'll discover even more people like them to serve (since you've clearly articulated who you help and how you help them)
6. You'll energize even more people with your vivid vision of the future and show them how to get there

And writing your book, creating your podcast—or both—is a great way to wrangle your thinking and wisdom into one place.

Where does it start?

Talk to people about the thing you're creating as you're creating it.

Your podcast or book will be done so much faster, and you'll be attracting more clients and partners sooner rather than later.

REFLECTION:
7 Triggers That Inspire People To Remember and Refer You

I f you've got something that will impact my business or life and help change the world, then make sure I understand it.

Let's say we've just met at a party, and I asked, *So, what do you do?*

What will you say?

Why would I want to spend some more time with you?

Why would I want to work, partner, or collaborate with you... or refer you to someone I know? Is there a partnership opportunity?

Whatever it is, make sure what you say is concise, compelling, and conversational—for you and me.

Here are seven thought triggers for what you offer. (I invite you to take your time and reflect on and take notes for each.)

1. Why are you doing what you do?
2. What have your audience, clients, customers, and colleagues shared about you and the results and outcomes you deliver (words, phrases, descriptions, results, outcomes, experience, benefits, etc.)?
3. Who do you serve? What do they want, and how/why do they want it?

4. What words will inspire them to choose what's good for them, for you, and for the planet?
5. What three words or phrases define you and how you work? Think simple, catchy, and memorable.
6. How would you explain it to a savvy fifteen-year-old?
7. Is there a story that captures the essence of why you do what you do?

Make sure people understand who you are, what you do, and why you do it. This is the cornerstone of service and how we can do more good for more people.

What Are You Discovering So Far?

Making Yes Easy

First, you are already an influencer. You're an expert. Remember that. Write that on the bathroom mirror. Next, remember that influence is simple. The greatest influencers have three things in common: their voice, what they know about their audience, and what they offer (that nobody else can).

1. So, become a person worth reading/listening to by speaking the language of the people you serve. Prove to your listeners, readers, and viewers that you are worth their investment of time and attention. And then their investment in your product or service.

2. Again, become a person worth reading/listening to by positioning yourself as a unique expert, authority, or thought leader with your message and business.

3. Leverage the idea or concept of what you're creating (book or podcast) *before* it's published or broadcast by having conversations with your potential clients and strategic partners.

And remember, your podcast being done means 80 percent of your book is done.

And vice versa.

Thanks to your podcast or book, there are lots of powerful, valuable ways that people can (and will) say yes to you and keep saying yes to you, like:

1. Choosing to visit your website, subscribe to your list, and open your emails
2. Clicking on your call-to-action, joining your webinar, and investing in your coaching, training, or product
3. Connecting with you on LinkedIn or contacting you for an interview
4. Hiring you for a leadership position or consultancy
5. Inviting you to speak or train (onstage or online)
6. Offering you a partnership or an appointment
7. Investing in your services or events
8. Doing your marketing for you by telling their colleagues, clients, and community all about you
9. Signing up for your mastermind or leadership program
10. Actually doing the work that will help them achieve the transformation they're looking for!

No matter who you are and what you do, these yeses are important because they will help move your business forward smartly and effectively.

Now, imagine how many lives you can impact with your ideas, message, vision, product, or service.

(And smile.)

The Many Voices of Story

S tories reach people's hearts and minds. That means your stories create inspiration by delivering an emotional experience to your reader or listener. While logic and facts are important, emotion moves people to action. Said another way: *Facts tell; emotions sell.* Stories make concepts and ideas real and tangible.

Stories connect the dots between the perceptual and conceptual parts of a person's experience.

It's one thing to hear or read the word fruit.

It's a completely different experience when you hear about, read, or see an image of a red apple in the hands of a smiling child getting ready to take another big bite… as the juice is already running down her chin.

Your stories invite people to see the world through your eyes and stand in your shoes. They also help get everyone on the same page with what's being communicated.

Stories (about you, about your clients, etc.) help people know you, like you, trust you, and want to develop an ongoing relationship with you. It's instant rapport with your audience, listener, or reader.

Thought Leadership and Your Special Sauce

Your story is an important part of who you are. Stories are the articulation of vision. Your story is part of your special sauce—your years of experience, education, "failures," triumphs, anecdotes, mishaps, insights, investment, wisdom, time, energy, effort, talent, and everything in between.

Your stories can include any/all of the following:

- Your signature story, mess-to-success moments, hard-earned wisdom, detours, and successes
- Case studies and testimonials
- Anecdotes about your colleagues, customers, clients, or audience
- Their successes, challenges, goals, and dreams
- Their experience of you or your company via your vision, idea, message, product, or service
- Relevant bits of the news/science/history/literature/popular culture/an interesting thing that happened to you last week
- Your purpose, guiding principles, and how you help make transformation and results happen

You have important stories. Your stories are key to what you offer to the world and the results you bring to people's businesses and lives. That's valuable stuff.

When you share your story, people will take an extra moment to read your words or hear what you're saying.

That's the power of story. Stories are key, whether teaching, coaching, selling, serving, training, speaking, or leading. Your story helps you connect the dots from your vision to people's goals and dreams.

Stories create opportunities for people to get to know you while positioning you as the expert, authority, or thought leader that you are.

1. This means that people will like you, trust you, and understand you care about them and their experience
2. They'll realize you truly see who they are, what they're dealing with, and what they most want to achieve
3. They'll know that you're the person who can help them get there, and they'll be delighted to say yes to you

Stories are good for your business. When you share them, here's what happens:

- You'll establish the connection from a person's head to their heart
- You'll inspire them to take action that's good for them, good for you, and (ideally) good for the world, too
- You'll have an audience that will hang onto your every word

We always use stories because they are the most direct way to bridge the gaps among different people. Especially in a world that's filled with so many different cultures, customs, countries, languages, dialects, geography, history, and politics.

- You can tell a story with an image or a picture, a handful of words, or even a 280-character tweet
- You can tell a story through video, email, or any communication medium that connects you to the people you serve
- You can tell a story instantly with a gesture or with your smile

With stories, you speak from the heart and connect with the hearts of the people near you, across the country, and around the world.

So, how are you using stories?

What We Think, Say, and Do

Everything humans create begins in the mind and heart. Inspiration and insight coupled with passion, intention, and the desire to bring things to life.

Put another way, what we think, say, and do create our reality (in that order). Uncountable numbers of scientists, leaders, athletes, spiritual masters, and high performers have proven this.

That's why so many people committed to achieving their goals and dreams dedicate time, energy, and intention to envisioning, affirming, and feeling their way to success.

Whether winning a gold medal, public speaking, writing a book, or self-healing, the power of affirmative thinking, imagination, and feeling is astounding. So is your reticular activating system.

In a nutshell, your reticular activating system is central to what you perceive in your consciousness. Like in a noisy room, you tune out the extra sounds and distractions so you can pay attention to what your friend is saying. It's what keeps the constant sensory input of the world in manageable bits. And it helps us stay focused on the ideas and actions that help you meet your goals and achieve your dreams.

So start using it right now:

1. Smile and breathe deeply. Let yourself relax from the top of your head to the tips of your toes. Take a few moments to connect to your unique sense of purpose.

2. Imagine you've succeeded in every way you want. Don't limit yourself. Allow all of it. What's your life like with your podcast or book done—or both? How does it feel?

 ✓ You're attracting more of the right leads, clients, and opportunities. And you're instantly positioned as an expert, authority, or thought leader in your market, industry, and field.
 ✓ That means you never have to worry about competing for business. And you get to wake up every day with freedom of your time, money, location, and creativity (as you define them).
 ✓ You have the privilege to share your message, make a difference, attract the money you want, and do it in a way that fits your business and lifestyle.

3. Feel the successes that are happening for you, your business, and the people you serve. Allow them to happen. If any fear, doubts, or hesitations come up, relax and let them go. Don't get involved.
4. Smile, breathe, and hold that beautiful, powerful vision and the feeling of the future for two or three breaths. Feel it feeling good in your body.
5. Now, visualize what you want to happen now (whether in the next three minutes, the next three months, or the next three years).

You're imprinting your subconscious with the images and feelings of the future you want.

Whether you're preparing to make an offer, learn a skill, play a game of tennis, or follow your morning ritual, imagine yourself doing it (successfully) *before* you do it. Because what you do and what you think about doing are the same thing as far, as your brain is concerned.

This is why Olympic athletes invest lots of time imagining themselves winning the gold.

Think of a high diver. She pictures herself making the perfect dive and entering the water without making a splash. She also pictures herself the moment the gold medal is placed around her neck. She can hear the resounding applause from the audience, and she feels a tear rolling down her cheek.

Your brain functions the same way. You can visualize your success by using as many of your five senses as possible and lots of emotion.

We invite you to take 60 seconds and try it out right now.

1. What's something you want to achieve?
2. When you're imagining it, what do you see?
3. What do you hear?
4. What do you taste or smell?
5. What can you feel in your body?
6. What are the emotions underneath as you imagine yourself experiencing success, reaching your goals, or achieving your dreams?
7. How do you picture yourself celebrating your success?

Pretty cool, right? You're remapping your brain and rewiring your subconscious mind. Now that you see how easy it is, below are three great times during your day for visualizing success.

- Before bed: Look back on your day. Smile and let yourself feel satisfied with what's happened. Make sure to account for at least seven instances of successes (big, small, in between).
- In the morning: Visualize having a successful day where you do great work, serve your people, and have lots of fun. Imagine your day moving seamlessly from one pleasant experience to the next. And that the challenges are totally doable and you can handle them easily.
- Before each segment of your day: Imagine quick, effective, enjoyable, and fulfilling success (client calls, being interviewed, writing your book, etc.). Anticipate any challenges as well as solutions to move beyond them.

All you need is just one to five minutes. Did you know? Five minutes = one-third of 1 percent of your day. That's only 0.35 percent of your day to craft your success and create the life you want.

While visualizing your future is key, you still want to spend most of your time here and now in the present moment. Mindful awareness and smiling meditation are great ways to be here now.

So keep building that 'muscle' of awareness, which is good for all things human.

Are You Meditating Yet?

More and more businesses are bringing meditation and mindfulness into the workplace, while more and more people are meditating at home and sharing awareness practices with their family, friends, and children.

Do a quick search on the web. You'll find articles on *CNN Money*, *Forbes*, *Huffington Post*, *Bloomberg Business*, and multiple reputable academic sources about meditation, mindful awareness, and how they contribute to success and happiness.

Meditation is the best gift for coaches, consultants, speakers, solopreneurs, small business owners, entrepreneurs, and leaders. Because it's been proven to help on all sorts of levels, including:

1. Staying healthier (mentally, physically, emotionally)
2. Being more flexible, creative, and innovative
3. Reducing anxiety, stress, doubt, and worry
4. Dealing with physical and emotional pain
5. Managing grief, impatience, and anger
6. Navigating change in a rapidly changing world
7. Being a better leader
8. Getting unstuck so you can get more of the right things done with less effort and less time

Ben's been studying meditation and meditating for over 20 years and has sat more than 130 days of silent retreat. The most effective type of meditation Ben has come across is metta (loving-kindness), as taught by the Buddha.

It's the fastest, most enjoyable, and easiest way to a lighter mind, open heart, and more happiness every day, regardless of the circumstances. And if you're so inclined, the practice of metta is a legitimate and effective path that has been helping people wake up for the last 2,600 years. (You don't need to be Buddhist or religious to enjoy the benefits. It even works for atheists and agnostics.)

Here's how to do metta (loving-kindness) mediation:

1. Close your eyes, sit comfortably, and allow yourself to breathe. Send yourself the sincere wish that you be happy and peaceful. Then think of a time when you were happy, and smile. (If that's difficult, imagine holding a puppy or a kitten in your arms.)

2. Notice the physical sensation in the center of your chest or heart area… like a warm, glowing, pleasant feeling.

3. Keep a tiny smile on your face and gently rest your awareness on that feeling or sensation of love in your heart. Do *not* try to concentrate. Keep breathing and smiling. Gently rest your awareness. Enjoy the feeling.

4. Then, allow that feeling to radiate out in all directions (no effort, just like the light of a candle). When you get distracted, which is normal, relax your head and face, smile, and return to the feeling of love in your heart. Keep breathing and smiling.

5. Keep practicing with no judgment and no striving. Just smile and breathe and relax with whatever comes up (whether on the cushion, in the car, at work, or just

living your life). Simply keep smiling and breathing and relaxing with whatever comes up. Keep letting go. Keep smiling and sending love.

This simple tool will help you unblock and unlock what's possible. "Because a light mind—is the right mind—to write." Say goodbye to stress with Smiling Meditation. Go here: InfluencersFormula.com/resources.

Part 5

Rocket-Ship Your Authority and Have the Business and Life You Want

False beliefs, forgiveness, and leadership lessons from Nelson Mandela. Plus, Donna and Ben's longer stories.

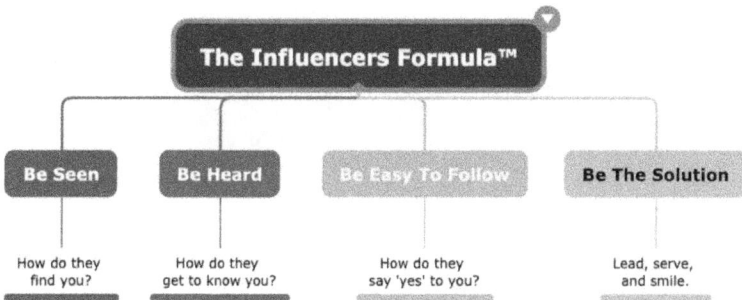

The Influencers Formula™

Be Seen	Be Heard	Be Easy To Follow	Be The Solution
How do they find you?	How do they get to know you?	How do they say 'yes' to you?	Lead, serve, and smile.

Letting Go of False Beliefs

The things we experience—with others, in the world around us, and with ourselves—are impacted by our interpretations, expectations, history, assumptions, intentions, beliefs, biology, principles, values, environment, associations, fears, and desires.

That's a lot of input that can keep us from seeing the truth and reality of the world around us and within ourselves.

For as much as we all must keep learning and understanding and discovering, there's as much, if not more, that we need to unlearn and release.

Wisdom, joy, and magic show up when we let things go.

Why? So we can grow, succeed, and create more positive impact in the world. And so we can love who we are and what we're about every single day.

Otherwise, our ability to make a bigger impact and live the life we love is limited by the roles, stories, and beliefs handed to us rather than what we've discovered for ourselves.

Did you ever stop and think about all the learning in your life? So much learning, so much information, so many experiences.

So much stuff holding you back from your greatness, your happiness, doing what you love (on your terms), and living your life you want.

These limiting factors may have come from:

- School
- Your family and friends
- TV
- Media
- The Internet
- Fake news
- Work
- Your mistakes and misperceptions
- Debt and scarcity thinking
- Religion and spirituality
- Altered states of consciousness
- Spouses or partners
- Your children
- Your pets
- Sickness, old age, or death

We all have values and beliefs we never chose for ourselves. But somehow, they became a part of us—and part of the business world. That's a lot from when you were young and very impressionable to today.

And that's what usually holds us back.

So what's one thing you can surrender right now? From there, what do you want to cultivate more of as you take your business (and life) to the next level?

Write it down and keep that list where you can see it.

(The bathroom mirror is a great place.)

A Leadership Lesson from Nelson Mandela

Nelson Mandela (affectionately known as "Madiba") was amazing. This wise being can teach us many things; a big one is about freedom. And how he responded to being locked up for twenty-seven years in a South African prison during apartheid.

The lesson is: No matter what happens, you can choose to respond instead of react.

Think about it. The ways people treat you (in the words of Yogi Bhajan) are a "reflection of the state of their relationship with themselves... rather than a statement about your value as a person."

That's a powerful truth.

And when you keep this truth on your radar, you immediately empower yourself.

You're able, from moment to moment, to respond rather than react and make smarter choices. You're influencing yourself to make more powerful and effective choices, more often.

For Madiba, this wasn't always easy. It was probably never easy. But he kept at it because he knew freedom starts on the inside.

After twenty-seven years in prison under the apartheid regime, he was elected president of South Africa in 1994.

We're all chock full of knee-jerk reactions just waiting to be unleashed—big ones, little ones, and everything-in-between ones.

But in those beautiful moments when you can choose to make a conscious choice and respond instead of react, you are creating freedom.

Freedom from these four things:

1. Reactions (even if only for a moment)
2. Habits (the ones that no longer serve you)
3. The past (regrets)
4. The future (worry and anxiety)

Freedom right now. Because this moment is filled with the seeds of possibility.

And the story continues...

When you take a few minutes to learn more about Madiba, you'll see something amazing. One person who let himself discover the gifts in the darkness. Gifts that led him to influence the course of history and an entire country.

And this leads us to the second thing I learned from Madiba: freedom is born from forgiveness.

In South Africa, apartheid meant that violence and human rights abuses were happening on all sides. No part of society escaped.

So South Africa took a revolutionary approach to healing: truth, reconciliation, and the possibility of forgiveness on a large scale (through their Truth and Reconciliation Commission).

The TRC offered public hearings where victims/survivors could share stories and possibly confront former abusers. There was an opportunity for both forgiveness and greater societal healing.

This powerful, national action proved that you can bring forgiveness into a larger arena. Because when you start forgiving others, you create more freedom for yourself.

- More forgiveness = more freedom
- More freedom = more power
- More power = more influence
- More influence = more impact

The Easiest and Best Way To Forgive

As you just discovered, forgiveness is critical to your freedom. Here's how to do it (and likely you've never done it this way before).

Instead of forgiving the specific words or actions or person, this approach is oriented on forgiving the "not understanding."

1. Sit quietly (eyes closed, a small smile on your face), make a strong intention to forgive yourself, and periodically repeat one of these phrases:

   I forgive myself for not *understanding* (i.e., making this/these mistake(s))

   or

   I forgive myself for causing pain to myself or anyone else

2. Then, shift your intention to another person. Again, periodically repeat the phrase *I forgive you for…*
3. Finally, imagine hearing the other person saying these words to you: *I forgive you for…*

Heads up! You may feel mental, physical, or emotional discomfort during this process. That's okay. Try not to take it personally or get caught up in a story.

Instead, relax your head and face and put that tiny smile back on your face. Take some breaths and let that mental fist unclench. Let your body relax. Keep smiling. Let your mind be lighter.

Repeat as necessary and allow changes to happen.

What Are You Discovering So Far?

Donna's Longer Story

I laugh when I think about it. Today, I'm a global radio authority and podcast expert. As of this writing, I've produced over 14,000 podcasts with three-quarters of a million downloads. But it wasn't always like this.

I was once a musician in the U.S. Army and had the honor of serving my country for 20 years. From there, I unexpectedly launched into retirement, sitting on the couch, waiting to die. I'd contracted Lyme disease from a tick bite, which left me physically and intellectually disabled.

Every part of me hurt.

It took me five years of procrastination to finally say yes to my dream of becoming a coach. Once I took the leap, I dived deep into learning everything I could about coaching, speaking, and training.

I thought, *Hey, if I'm going to be miserable and stuck on the couch, this could at least give me something productive to do.* Once I finally said yes to my dream, it took no time to launch my coaching practice. I hit the ground running and never looked back. I found a new joy and passion in coaching—so much so that I became a bit of a learning junkie. I took as many coaching courses and certifications as I could find. (Hooray for the GI Bill and time on my hands!).

Then, after I sent my youngest off to college, I had a funny realization: I'd created a vision board in one of my classes, and I noticed a row of microphones at the top.

Suddenly, everything else dropped away. It stopped me in my tracks because I was always told to "be seen and not heard" when I was growing up.

Speaking up, in a bigger way, felt scary. And the idea of using a microphone to speak intimidated me.

However, I decided to lean into the universe's message, and I realized that there was something profound about those microphones. They became an invitation to step out of my comfort zone and explore the power of my voice.

Then, I intentionally began creating opportunities to sit behind a microphone. It started with being an emcee at a chamber event, and things took off from there. I landed a spot on a local radio station promoting the event. Before I knew it, I cohosted several shows. The unexpected twists and turns eventually led to a partnership, allowing us to start our internet radio station during the challenging times of the COVID.

Saying yes to unexpected microphone opportunities has been a game-changer throughout this journey. Despite moments of doubt and imposter syndrome, stepping out of my comfort zone has led to remarkable accomplishments:

- Receiving the Maxwell Lead and Lift Others Culture Award
- Being recognized by the Commonwealth of Virginia House of Delegates as one of the Top 50 Women Leaders of Virginia
- My first book!

If you had told me seven years ago that I would be a podcast producer of over 14,000 podcasts (with over three-quarters of a million downloads) and co-founder of IBGR.network, I would never have believed you. Now, I deliver worldwide transformation every single day. I've experienced firsthand the incredible potential we all carry within.

I hope my story will encourage you to explore the possibilities in your life and business. And see how they can align with your journey to embrace your voice, amplify your message, and inspire change in your unique way.

You never know where it might lead you!

Ben's Longer Story

I 'd like to take just a few minutes and tell you my story. Because I'd like you to know who I am, where I've been, and what I'm about. And to let you know where my insights and discoveries have come from.

So I invite you to take a moment, take a deep breath, smile, and imagine me trekking in the mountains of southern India with a guide named Vijay (who had a huge smile).

At 6,000 feet, it was hot, dry, and dusty because it hadn't rained in four months. The sun was beating down on our heads and shoulders, and Vijay shared his story as we walked along the path.

Suddenly, from somewhere behind the trees, I could hear screams and shouts (not in English, of course). And then Vijay yelled, "Run!" over his shoulder as he ran down the path.

So, I ran. And ran. And ran.

I didn't know why I was running, but I knew I was running for my life.

And this was the second time—out of four times in 72 hours—that I almost died in India. As I kept running along this dry and dusty mountain path, my life flashed before my eyes.

I remembered my childhood, then high school in New York City (mostly), and college, where I earned a BA in psychology and creative writing.

I remembered producing magazines published by Hearst and Condé Nast, working with multiple startups, and traveling around the world.

I remembered helping launch *AARP The Magazine*, which was mailed to 32 million people.

I remembered helping two chapters of The ALS Association through an organizational consolidation so they could serve half the people in California living with Lou Gehrig's disease (a few years before The Ice Bucket Challenge). Not to mention creating their first mindfulness program for patients and their families.

Then I remembered being fed up:

- Tired of the business world because everything I could see was focused on profit at the expense of everything and everyone else.
- Discouraged by nonprofits because I could see that most didn't have the power, knowledge, training, or resources to make a bigger impact (even though so many nonprofits and NGOs do incredible things).

That's when it dawned on me. I want to make an ongoing, major, positive shift on the planet. So I chose to help the individuals, organizations, and movements already making a difference: those that want to turn up the volume on their influence, income, and impact.

With this clarity, I focused on becoming a top-notch leader, coach, marketer, and communicator. I also started a regular meditation practice that I've been doing since 2006 (including over 130 days of silent retreats so far).

I spent years synthesizing everything I'd learned, created, and achieved (at school and in the corporate world, nonprofit world, and my life). I studied with incredible coaches. I joined masterminds with influential people and learned from powerful mentors. I analyzed genius copywriters. I read tons of books, took lots of courses, and took pages and pages and pages of notes.

The more I learned, the more action I took. More action meant more feedback; more feedback meant more clarity. More clarity meant more results.

I also made lots (and lots) of mistakes. So, I reflected on all of these "failures," learned the lessons (some tough ones), and integrated my wisdom and insights.

Today, I'm a four-time, best-selling author, podcast, and international radio show host. My teachings are used by more than 80,000 leaders and game-changers around the world. I help folks write great books in as little as five weeks, enjoy five-figure speaking fees, and attract six-figure consulting. (That's before they even publish.)

I've trained hundreds of millionaires and helped a Fortune 100 create an empathy video game for 20,000 employees. With 39 years of writing and publishing adventures, I helped launch the world's largest magazine *(AARP)* and received a patient services award from The ALS Association.

And that's what's up at the time of this writing.

Let's see what happens next!

Part 6

The Influencers Formula™ Roadmap (for podcasts, books, and TV talk shows)

Business podcasting made easy, writing your book faster than the average bear, and how to skip paying your publisher an extra $180,000. Plus the million-dollar timeline, how to choose your best stories, and making sure your podcast (or book) will work.

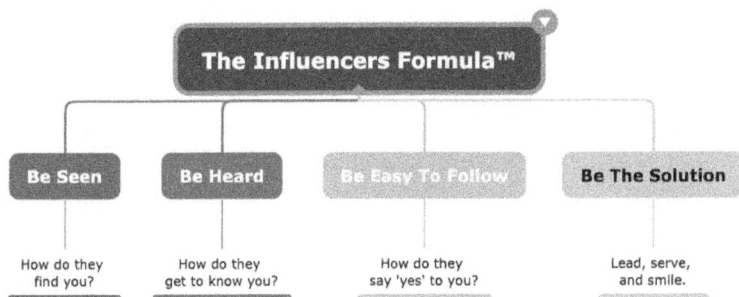

The Influencers Formula™

Be Seen	Be Heard	Be Easy To Follow	Be The Solution
How do they find you?	How do they get to know you?	How do they say 'yes' to you?	Lead, serve, and smile.

Rocket-Ship Your Authority and Have the Business and Life You Want

As you've already discovered, The Influencers Formula™ Roadmap (IFR) is the path to instant expertise and thought leadership with a podcast, book, or TV talk show you're proud of. The IFR is for:

- Leaders, consultants, coaches, speakers, entrepreneurs, solopreneurs, and small business owners who want to amplify their income, influence, and impact
- The 87 percent of brilliant entrepreneurs are not (yet) sustainably making six or seven figures
- People who understand the power of starting their marketing, partnering, and revenue generation... long before the podcast or book is published (or even finished)
- People who don't want to die with their story inside
- You, if you want to live your life without regrets

So we invite you to use the Formula to rocket-ship your authority and have the business and life you want (without getting derailed by the "stuff" that stops most people).

This includes where to start, how to publish (without having to sell your children), fear, doubt, imposter syndrome, a misperceived "lack" of time, and so much more).

All this "stuff" is perfectly normal and natural, albeit often tedious and unpleasant. So again, relax your head, relax your face, and smile. Keep breathing and smiling. Keep relaxing into what comes up, don't take any of it personally, and keep letting go.

Whether it's a podcast, book, or TV talk show, the first thing you want to do is to be seen.

Sadly, too many brilliant, meaningful, life-changing stories become long-forgotten history because most people die with their stories inside. Most of us hide away instead of sharing our knowledge, expertise, and experience. Many of us never take that first step to speak our truth and reason for being here. And so, we're just left in those last moments asking, *Why didn't I?*

(That is one of the top five regrets of the dying, after all.)

So don't die with your story inside; take your shot because people need you right now.

When you put The Influencers Formula™ Roadmap into action, you automatically brand/position yourself and your business right, attracting more ideal leads and clients sooner and faster.

Make sense?

Here's The Influencers Formula™ Roadmap in more detail.

Be seen

- Have a clear and consistent brand
- Move quickly, but don't rush
- Keep letting go of what's in the way

Be heard

- Keep speaking with your ideal clients and strategic partners
- Stand out as an expert, authority, or thought leader with your message
- Share your authentic voice

Be easy to follow

- Connect the dots and make yes easy
- Amplify, elevate, and repurpose
- Make use of the champagne glass pyramid

Be the solution

- Lead like never before
- Serve your best people
- Don't die with your story inside

Now, keep reading (or listening) to see how easy it is to choose thirteen of your best stories.

How to Choose 13 of Your Best Stories

As you already discovered, story and stories can mean:

- Your signature story, mess-to-success moments, hard-earned wisdom, detours, and successes
- Case studies and testimonials
- Anecdotes about your colleagues, customers, clients, or audience
- Their successes, challenges, goals, and dreams
- Their experience of you or your company via your vision, idea, message, product, or service
- Relevant bits of the news/science/history/literature/popular culture/an interesting thing that happened to you last week, etc.
- Your purpose, guiding principles, and how you help make transformation and results happen

How do you choose stories? Try this:

1. Choose three stories about yourself that indicate you are a reliable source of information and a go-to person in your field.
2. Come up with five brief anecdotes or illustrations that connect the dots from who you are and what you offer to the outcomes people want.

3. Think of all your unique stories. What story can you share that expresses you—the unique and wonderful you?

4. Capture a story that helped inspire your purpose or speaks to the beautiful heart that you have.

5. Select your three biggest professional successes and write about them in a way that shows tangible outcomes. As you articulate any of these stories, draw upon other aspects of your life, whether personal, professional, or anything in between (without compromising your privacy, of course).

This means:

- Make your stories multi-sensory (use as many of the five senses, plus emotion, as possible). You'll want to *show* and *tell*.

- Tell your reader, audience, or listener about the picture you just painted for them.

- Speak, write, and connect from your heart and mind. To do this, simply become aware of or put your hand over your heart for a moment. Smile and breathe.

- Keep a file of these stories available and accessible.

- And then watch to see how you impact people's lives.

Now that you know the Roadmap and have some stories in mind, keep reading to discover all sorts of goodies about podcasts.

The Influencers Formula™ Roadmap—Business Podcasting Made Easy

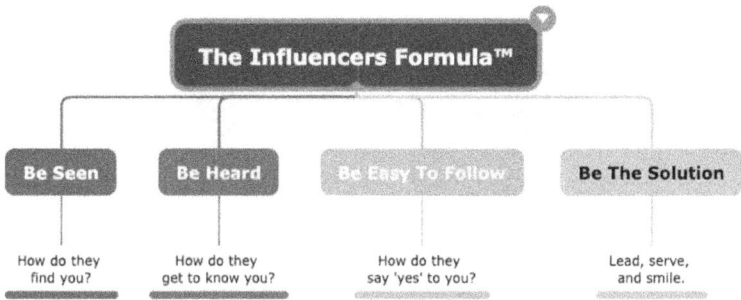

The Influencers Formula™

Be Seen	Be Heard	Be Easy To Follow	Be The Solution
How do they find you?	How do they get to know you?	How do they say 'yes' to you?	Lead, serve, and smile.

As we shared before, Donna is wild about the power of the podcast/global radio show combination because it's how she helps hosts attract new listeners while creating a radio show that instantly becomes a podcast (and also happens to be 80 percent of their book done).

Not to mention that a podcast is one of the best ways to amplify your voice, message, and impact.

Did you know? There's a 97 percent chance that a podcast is good for *your* business because:

- With the market size a staggering $23 billion, the podcasting world is thriving like never before. There are 464.7 million podcast listeners globally as of 2023, and it is predicted to reach 504.9 million by 2024.
- People listen in over 150 languages. And it's not just audio anymore. Video podcast production is now at an all-time high, offering listeners a visual and immersive experience.
- The United States boasts the highest number of podcast listeners worldwide, with over 100 million active listeners as of this writing.
- Podcasts are part of people's daily routine, with almost 1/3 of the entire US tuning in weekly.

– Source: Demand Sage

Even with all the great reasons already mentioned, there are some common roadblocks with podcasts that keep most people stuck:

1. [Fear] *What if I make a mistake? What if I sound stupid? I don't have anything worth sharing that hasn't been done already.*
2. [Perfectionism] Because it kills progress and real-time feedback.
3. [Audience] Do you know who your people are, what they want, and how to communicate with them? Are they already investing in you?
4. [Tech] *I'm not savvy. It's overwhelming. I don't know what I need, so I don't want to waste money. What if I get hacked?*
5. [Time and Money] *How do I know it's worth it?* (HINT: You'll know it's worth it if you're having conversations with your ideal clients about the podcast you're creating as you're creating it.)

Now, imagine what your business and life would be like if you could reach hundreds of thousands of engaged listeners—who are also your ideal clients.

That's what you can do with a podcast.

Here's how:

[FIRST] Mic your message (and get noticed)

- Have conversations with your ideal clients/audience
- Follow a proven roadmap and create your 13 weeks of show notes

[SECOND] Mic your method (broadcasting and structure)

- Choose the right equipment and platforms
- Structure your show. Will you do it solo, interview style, or with a cohost?

[THIRD] Mic your marketing (amplify your message, income, and impact)

- Build or grow your audience following The Influencers Formula™ Roadmap: be seen, be heard, be easy to follow, and be the solution
- Monetize your show by building strategic partners and leveraging your content
- Keep serving your best audience

(In case you're wondering, mic is short for microphone.)

With this handy resource, you'll have everything you need… from idea to broadcast. Includes roadmap and audio training. Go here for Business Podcasting Made Easy: InfluencersFormula.com/resources.

Writing Profitable Show Notes

I magine not even having to think about what goes where for your podcast.

The Profitable Show Notes framework is the easiest way to get your podcast out of your head. And good news! You'll write your podcast show notes with the *intention* of leveraging and repurposing them.

That's what makes what we're doing with The Influencers Formula™ Roadmap so unique and powerful. You can create a year's worth of podcasts (52 episodes) in one financial quarter!

Your Profitable Show Notes Framework has six components. Here's what they are, and here's how to get writing right away:

1. Write your episode title, which is the episode promise. Because most of the time, your listeners will listen with their eyes... before they listen with their ears.
2. Next, add a hook. The hook can be a quote, a short statistic, or a few lines from a story that will serve as a showstopper.
3. Then, you tell them "why." Write a sentence that lets your listener know why this topic is important. What is the benefit for them?
4. From there, it's the "what." What's the context? Here's the knowledge and information part of it. What do you want your listeners to know? (Such as background,

science, data hearsay in the news according to your results/outcomes, etc.)

5. "How?" What do you want your listeners to do? What must they do to have the results you promised in the episode title? Share all the steps you want them to take.

6. "What if?" Help your listener imagine how their business or life will be elevated by doing what you're teaching. Then, make it easy for them to take the first step.

Show notes (and episodes) are easy to create with this framework. Always return to your promise. You want just enough for the eyes to tell the ears to listen. We recommend one bullet point/sentence for each of the six components.

Not only that.

If you map out your podcast and use the framework above, you can easily apply most of that map to your book. (As long as you're making sure to have conversations with your ideal clients, as you're creating your content.)

The Influencers Formula™ Roadmap—How to Write Your Book Faster than the Average Bear

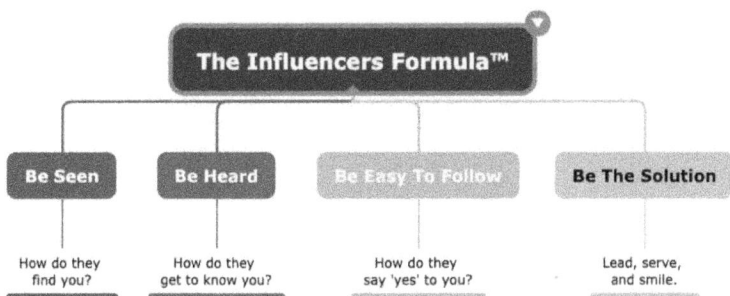

The Influencers Formula™

Be Seen	Be Heard	Be Easy To Follow	Be The Solution
How do they find you?	How do they get to know you?	How do they say 'yes' to you?	Lead, serve, and smile.

There are three keys to writing your book faster than the average bear. Now, we're not talking about a novel, fiction, or a book of poetry.

We're talking about the kind of book that positions you as an expert in your field and helps you bring your message to the world. Some people might get concerned when they hear the word expert.

You don't have to be *the* expert.

You simply want to be a world-class expert in your stuff because nobody can do what you do. Nobody can teach what you teach. Nobody can deliver what you deliver because of your amazing skills, experience, and expertise.

Case Study: Books Change Lives

OPPORTUNITY — I (Ben) was invited to teach a two-day training at Stanford University about the Influence with a Heart Method®. The audience was 126 seven-figure-earning global business leaders.

BACKGROUND — I knew I needed to make an extra good impression, so I told the event planner I would give each person a free, autographed copy of my new book.

SOLUTION — I wrote my book in five weeks and arrived at the event with copies in hand.

RESULTS — New business came my way almost immediately. One audience member discovered that I was coming to Australia later that year as a guest speaker at a different event on the Sunshine Coast. He invited me to speak at their company headquarters in Sydney. Two days later, he asked me to do a second talk (the next day) to a Chinese-speaking audience through a translator.

Next, I'm confirming a six-figure contract with a Fortune 100 company three months later. They'd asked me to help create a mindfulness and empathy video game with MIT for more than 20,000 customer experience employees around the world.

So, like we said, this kind of book positions you as an expert in your field so you can attract the right opportunities as you bring your message to the world. And the cool thing is that you can start making a bigger impact and attracting more clients even before your book is published. (Even before your book is written, for that matter.) And that's pretty cool!

Here are the three keys:

1. The first key is to choose a book length ahead of time. So rather than writing into the abyss and not knowing when you will finish, not knowing what to write, and when to stop, you choose ahead of time.
2. The second key is to write as little as possible. Now, that might sound funny because you're writing a book. But the magic here is to dictate (for at least some of your book). Because you don't waste time thinking, editing, and judging yourself or your words. Just be the expert you are. And dictating means that your authentic voice will be coming through. Not to mention 1,200 words every seven minutes. That's 5 percent of your book!
3. The third key is to start as soon as possible. But don't rush. (Ben sometimes talks about being a

hospice volunteer and getting that smart, stark gift and reminder that life is uncertain. There's no guarantee that we will make it until tomorrow or even until our next breath.)Get moving and stay present.

So now is the time to make it happen. And we invite you to say yes to yourself. Because when you say yes, the whole universe begins to conspire to help you make your dreams into reality. (Whether that's spiritual, quantum physics, your reticular activation system, sweat equity—or all four—it works.)

Best Math Quiz Ever

How many books do you have to sell to make $100,000? If you're working with a traditional publisher (which we DON'T recommend), you have to sell 80,000 to 100,000!

But the better answer may surprise you.

It's zero!

How?

Use your book to develop relationships with 1 to 20 people who can get you to that $100,000 goal much faster.

Why spend time, money, and energy trying to sell a bunch of books?

Use your book to cultivate relationships that will bring more income, influence, and impact so much faster!

The 5 Biggest Book Mistakes

We would love for you to bring your book to the world. We would love for you to share your message, make the impact you want to make, get the clients you want, and have the life you want.

Your book is a brilliant way to do that. But so many folks don't write their book. Many more don't finish their book. And some finish their book, but the book disappears into obscurity, and nobody gets the benefit.

This is very sad.

So, stop the madness—right now. The beautiful opportunity is that when you know the mistakes, you don't have to make them anymore, or you can avoid them in the first place.

The five biggest book mistakes are so easy to avoid, yet they literally cost people millions of dollars a year and decades of life.

Here they are:

1. Not knowing your audience. Most people don't understand their audience's needs and wants and don't use their language. This happens when you don't take the time to ask questions and listen.
2. Not sharing stories. Most people don't include stories about themselves. They don't include case studies; they don't include what happened on the bus the other day—none of the goodness that makes books (and you) memorable.

3. Not using a schedule. Most people don't put 'book time' on their calendar; it simply remains a someday thing that eats away at their joy and willpower. Life is so much easier when you put stuff on the calendar.
4. Old-school thinking. There is no such thing as writer's block. And you can bring your message to the world without needing a traditional publisher. (Professional self-publishing is the way to go.)
5. (Just) Writing. The last big mistake that people make is they actually try to write their book! Instead, it's better, faster, easier, and smarter to dictate your book so you can get it done right, in your voice.

That's it. Now you know.

Because when you know the mistakes, you don't have to make them anymore.

Or you can just avoid them in the first place.

The book quiz, coming up in a few pages, will help.

The Million-Dollar Book Timeline and Strategy

When Ben wrote his second book in three weeks (before speaking at Stanford), he used this timeline and strategy, which launched his entire business.

Here is the million-dollar book launch timeline and strategy. When you put it in place, you can (for example) get your book into the hands of 100 of your ideal clients.

How will your business change if just one to five of them (1 percent to 5 percent) invest in your high-ticket offer?

It's the simplest six-, seven- and eight-figure activity that you can do with your book.

Here's the timeline and strategy:

1. Write your book (in one to six months at two to six hours a week)
2. Editing, design, and production (three months)
3. On-sale date/book available to buy [date]
4. Smart gap here (two to nine months)
5. Bestseller launch date [date]

Here's how it works:

1. The first thing is to get your book done. For Ben's authors—who are using dictation, a blueprint, a process, and a timeline—they spend about three hours weekly for 13 weeks. You can do it faster if you want.

2. When you hand in your final or almost-final manuscript, the editing, design, and production will happen. Make sure to give yourself and your publisher three months to complete the process. Give yourself the time. Sometimes, when the book is being edited, you may realize, *Oh snap! I forgot an entire section*—even after all of the outlining and writing! Or you have great new insight or an incredible case study thanks to a new client. Give yourself the space and spaciousness to get the book done right.

3. Next, get your book up for sale. Let's say it's on September 1. Make it available on that date. BUT do *not* do your bestseller launch on September 1, September 2, or even September 3, for that matter. Simply release the book and do whatever kind of marketing is strategic for now.

4. From there, wait at least two months before doing your bestseller book launch.

5. Use this smart gap to take a rest and celebrate! You can do marketing if you want to. You can get copies and send them to all your friends, business associates, leads, clients, and potential partners. You want to develop relationships with people. How will your business change if just one of them invests in a next step with you?

Then, imagine getting your book into the hands of 100 of your ideal clients, and five of them (5 percent) invest in your high-ticket offer...

That's the power and potential of your book!

Quiz: Will Your Book Actually Work?

This is a quiz that's good for your business. That means it's time to take a good, hard, loving look at your book (or the book you think you want to write now). On a scale of 1 to 10, how important are these for your book?

(10 = SUPER IMPORTANT)

1. Your book inspires *and* informs. _____
2. The title of your book makes your ideal clients stop and pay attention. _____
3. Your book gains you instant trust because your reader feels you're "just like family." _____
4. Your readers want to contact you and become clients before reaching your table of contents. _____
5. Your book is easy to read and hard to forget because it's written for skimmers, scanners, AND people who read all the way through. _____
6. You know what makes your ideal clients/readers/audience tick. _____
7. You seed your offer throughout your book without sounding like a sleazy, used car salesman. _____
8. The pages and sections about you are relevant, unforgettable, and authentic. _____

9. Your book happily sets your readers on the path to your high ticket offer—even if they've just "met you" in the pages of your book. _____
10. Your book offers timeless wisdom, universal human truths, and valuable information. _____
11. Your book is already positioning you the right way and making you money (even if it's still not finished). _____

What did you discover? Are you clear about your book actually working?

We invite you to book a quick call with Ben, and he'll help you get clear.

Visit <u>influencewithaheart/chat</u> today.

What Are You Discovering
So Far?

_____

_____

_____

_____

_____

_____

_____

_____

_____

_____

_____

_____

_____

_____

_____

_____

_____

_____

_____

_____

_____

_____

The Influencers Formula™ Roadmap—Demystifying Publishing and Launching Your Book (with our thanks to Chris O'Byrne)

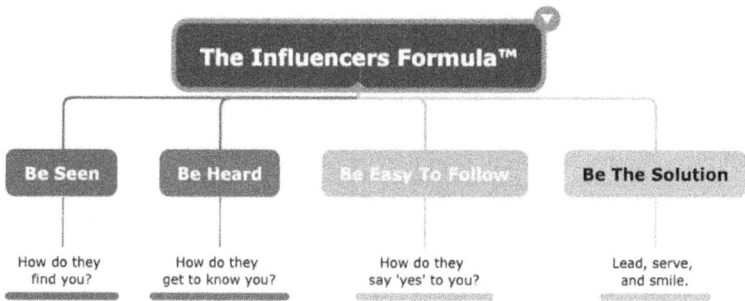

The Influencers Formula™

Be Seen	Be Heard	Be Easy To Follow	Be The Solution
How do they find you?	How do they get to know you?	How do they say 'yes' to you?	Lead, serve, and smile.

I magine what your life is like with your book done. You have a high-quality published book, bringing you leads, clients, and opportunities. It instantly positions you as an expert in your market, industry, or field. You never have to worry about competing for business.

You are the expert—the thought leader. You've written the book. And you get to wake up every day with freedom (as you define it). You get to share your message, make a difference, attract all the money you want, and do it in a way that fits your life and lifestyle.

If you want to create the book you want that will transform your business and life, pay extra attention to what we're about to share. Because publishing success comes from understanding how the process works so you can walk across the publishing finish line with ease.

The illustrious Charles Bukowski once talked about how a lot of publishing is done through things like politics, friends, and natural stupidity.

Let's avoid all of that. (No offense to anyone's friends.)

Did you know? You no longer need a traditional publisher to be a successful published author. It's great news and especially important because there's a good chance that book sales (by themselves) will get you nowhere.

More great news: you have more freedom, control, and resources to create the book you want on your terms. You don't have to give up your intellectual property, and there's no need to become contractually obligated (to a traditional publisher) to buy thousands of books (that end up in your garage).

Working with a traditional publisher is like betting against the house. When you visit a casino, you might experience the benefits up front, but in the long run, the house always wins.

Instead, thanks to professional self-publishing, you can have your book written and published in four to seven months (rather than one, two, or more years), which is common in traditional publishing.

So here's your chance to do it right.

But how do you know who to trust?

Talk to folks. Ask for referrals. Look at reviews of the people you're interested in working with. Make sure you know exactly what you'll receive, get it in writing, and be crystal clear before signing or paying.

Trust your gut. Don't negate that.

Make sure you understand the strategy for *your* book because most publishers don't do anything other than publishing.

Many authors make the expensive mistake of choosing incomplete, high-cost, low-value publishing.

For the kind of book you want to bring into the world, you'll want a complete solution for your book instead. That means business development, target market, book writing, client attraction, publishing, marketing, launching, and leveraging.

If you want to stand out as an expert and make a bigger impact with your message, this is the way to go because it keeps you focused on your book, brand, and business all at once.

But What About My Book Advance?

Watch out for old-school thinking like, *It's better to be traditionally published than self-published.*

That's not the case 99 percent of the time.

Keep in mind that a traditional publisher is operating a business. Their goal is to sell as many books as possible.

There's nothing wrong with that, other than it just doesn't serve you.

A traditional publisher is going to minimize risks and conserve as much cash as possible. That's how they make their money.

- This is why they take 90 percent or more in royalties
- This is why you most likely won't get an advance
- This is why they don't do the marketing

As we've shared, working with a traditional publisher is like betting against the house. When you visit a casino, you might experience the benefits up front, but in the long run, the house always wins.

Here's what to expect from a traditional publisher:

1. You sign away all the rights to your book (your intellectual property). They own it, and they can do whatever they want with it.
2. They can change the content. And rarely do you have any input into the cover design or the final manuscript.
3. They often choose the title.

But you say, "What about my advance?"

Traditional publishing has changed. Almost nobody gets an advance these days, and the amounts are small for those who do. Publishers won't give you an advance if they don't know if they can sell your books.

(Because most books from traditional publishers are essentially educated guesses for what might work. Or might not.)

Yes, some people get that million-dollar advance. But those folks have a big audience or following and are almost guaranteed to sell a million dollars' worth of books.

On top of that, you usually can't submit your manuscript directly to a publisher. You must go through a literary agent (who will, by the way, also take a percentage of your royalties). That means you must find an agent who's even interested in your book in the first place because they all have a vetting process.

And then, if the agent decides to take you on, you will need to write a proposal, essentially a thirty-five-page sales letter, selling your book to publishers.

Why go anywhere near that mess?

Do you want to give up your creative freedom and the rights to your intellectual property?

Do you want someone (other than you) to change your message?

Or your voice?

Imagine the terrible feeling of putting all that effort into writing something real, true, and authentic to you, and someone changes it.

Yuck.

You don't need permission, approval, or anything from a publisher. The only people you need to resonate with are your ideal clients.

Can I Just Use AI to Write my Book?

Artificial intelligence in the form of tools like ChatGPT can be very useful. It's a powerful tool you can use to help you with all aspects of your writing, from articles to emails.

However, it can't replace you and your unique brain. It can help you brainstorm ideas, create an outline, or get your creativity flowing. But it can't replace you and your unique and wonderful mind.

Don't be afraid to use your own voice. You might think you have nothing unique to say, but that's not true. Every time you speak or think, you are being unique. You have your own wonderful combination that is you.

Stop being afraid to be you. Stop being afraid to use your unique voice. You have a unique and wonderful message to share. In fact, you have many messages to share. Even making the decision of which message you want to share and when and where is unique to you.

Use AI as a tool, a supplement, but don't try to make it a replacement for you. Because it can't. No thing and nobody can replace you.

Sell Thousands of Books or Pay Thousands of Dollars

T hen there's the much-too-common story of an author who went with one of the big publishers. Their contract stipulated that the author had to sell 10,000 copies or buy the remainder at full price.

Think about it: You write a book. Let's say you manage to sell 1,000 of those books; great. But now you have 9,000 more books that you are contracted to buy at full cost, which could be $20 per book. So, we're talking about potentially 9,000 X $20 = $180,000.

That means that you owe the publisher $180,000. And for this privilege, they will take about 90 percent of your royalties on top of it.

How to Have Control of Your Book

You have complete control when you professionally self-publish. Just make sure you're working with a professional. Yes, we're emphasizing that you get professional help.

The big mistake people make is trying to save money by doing this on their own. Another big mistake is when people launch a book immediately after their book is available for sale.

Depending on the approach to producing and publishing a book, there are 400–700 pieces to the puzzle.

That is not for you. Your job is to get clients, serve your clients, and speak to people to get more clients, helping more people.

When to Launch Your Book

The truth is, you can launch your book at any time, and you can launch your book more than once (i.e., for your ebook, then print book, and then audiobook.)

And if you're smart (and we know you are), you will do your bestseller launch two to nine months after your book is released (available for sale). Here's why:

1. You just completed your book, hooray! Take a rest. Take a breather. It's time to celebrate. (Yes, you can start marketing the book after resting; just don't launch yet.)

2. Take the time between the release date and the bestseller launch date to develop relationships with potential partners. Get on podcasts or devote several of your podcast episodes to your book.

3. See if you can teach some of your book content as a masterclass or LinkedIn audio to someone else's audience.

Here's exactly what to do (and when) so you can become a bestselling author and cultivate relationships that amplify your income, influence, and impact. Go here to know what to do before, during, and after your book launch: InfluencersFormula.com/resources.

The Influencers Formula™ Roadmap—TV Talk Shows

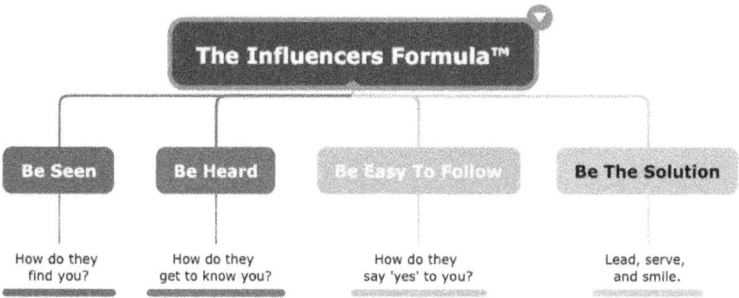

The Influencers Formula™

Be Seen	Be Heard	Be Easy To Follow	Be The Solution
How do they find you?	How do they get to know you?	How do they say 'yes' to you?	Lead, serve, and smile.

W e've learned something important from the teachings and wisdom of Declan Oceguera, creator of the TV TalkShow Formula: if you're not findable on video these days, you're missing out.

Here are some reasons why it's time to unleash your authority and elevate your visibility as a thought leader with video

1. In recent surveys of the video industry, 84 percent of the people surveyed (almost everyone) said that they were convinced to buy something because they watched a video.
2. Even more people said they would watch a video before they make a buying decision.
3. These days, people spend more time watching online videos than traditional TV or cable programming.

That's huge.

And it makes perfect sense.

Because we all watch videos all the time, and then we often buy things because we're familiar with what we've seen on a screen (like a commercial, a review, or a how-to video).

People are now spending far more time watching video content online; computers, phones, tablets, and YouTube on TV are just a few examples.

All of that is technically called TV now.

A great way to be findable is with a TV talk show.

A TV talk show is an online video interview format that features you as the host (or you and someone else as a cohost).

The TV talk show format allows you to amplify your visibility and attract a wider audience that may not engage with podcasts or books. Hosting a TV talk show also allows you to grow your network by connecting with guests and accessing their sphere of influence.

Additionally, using video as part of your marketing helps you reach more people and ultimately attract more clients and strategic partners.

Along with books and podcasts, video creates comprehensive visibility that elevates and amplifies your message.

Like a talk show you've seen on traditional TV, your show will have a theme. Each episode will explore some aspect of your theme through the discussions you're having with your guest, your cohost, or even if it's you solo.

Don't forget your target audience.

Who are you for? You're not for everybody. And you're not meant to be.

But you are for a specific group of people who resonate with you and your expertise.

That means video can support your income, influence, and impact by:

1. Expanding your visibility and connecting with people who enjoy videos.
2. Serving more of the right people and repelling those who aren't a fit.
3. Tapping into other people's networks and expanding your reach beyond your existing connections.
4. Elevating and solidifying your expertise and credibility.
5. Getting ahead of the curve: Embracing the TV-talk-show format gives you a huge advantage in reaching your audience through video.

6. Attracting more leads: Hosting a TV talk show generates more conversations and word-of-mouth referrals, leading to potential clients and business opportunities. Not to mention the instant platform and tons of marketing content.

7. Engaging with your audience, sharing your message with the world, and enjoying it (even if you're hesitant at first).

The Evolution of Television

The concept of TV that many of us grew up with has morphed. TV is now any form of live-streamed or pre-recorded video or video-based content, regardless of how that content is accessed. That's a powerful shift in TV, and that's great news for you.

You can easily become a TV talk show host.

This is good because, in the last couple of years, savvy podcasters and authors have been incorporating more video into their marketing and platform.

But Will People Actually Listen To What I Say?

Yes.

Here's how to make sure.

Simply have conversations with your ideal clients about the TV talk show you're creating.

Then you'll know exactly what to say.

But stay alert!

Because when your inner critic starts rearing its ugly head, practice relaxing, breathing, smiling, and letting go of those stories and false beliefs.

- "I'm too old."
- "I'm too fat."
- "I'm too this."
- "I'm too that."
- "I'm too short."
- "It's too late."
- "I'm too new."
- "I can't stand the way I look on camera."
- "My hair and makeup aren't right."
- "Oh, my goodness, the lights!"
- "I don't know what to say."
- "What if no one cares?"

What If They Do Care?

What if just ten people cared? And it changed their lives? And then they told ten people? And then they told ten people?

What would happen for you, your business, and all those lives you touch directly and indirectly?

Consider this when it comes to making videos or having a TV talk show that you know allows you to be seen and heard.

You have a certain bubble of existence right now, which may include thoughts and beliefs that it's not okay for you to be seen and heard, that it's not okay for you to be that visible or vulnerable. So, your bubble right now might be, "That's not for me." Exactly. You might think it could be, but your bubble says, "Nope, you can't do that." Do you want to know how to stop that?

Decide who you are willing to be to produce extraordinary results. Write three words that describe the person you are willing to be. Tape them to your bathroom mirror and repeat daily, *I am…*

And in the meantime, we invite you to start/keep using video to attract more clients and strategic partners while making a bigger impact with your message.

Here are five things to consider:

1. When thinking about your TV talk show, it should align with the theme of your book or podcast, whether you've already written the book or have plans to do so. Take a moment to jot down something related to your area of expertise. This theme will serve as your starting point.
2. Make a list of your ten dream guests. Connect with them on LinkedIn directly. And/or see who they're connected to and see if you can be introduced.
3. Now, what's your intention? (For example, Declan has a show called *The Visionary Voyager,* where he inspires people to live their dreams through travel.)
4. Next, identify (or clarify) your audience. Who are the best people for your show? Do you know their demographics, interests, and aspirations? Do you know the language they use? What are their biggest challenges, goals, and dreams?
5. What's the promise of your show? What will you deliver to your audience during each episode? Is it aligned with your intention? Do your viewers actually want it?

Take a moment to reflect on these aspects and let your ideas flow. This process will provide a solid foundation for your

TV talk show, ensuring it aligns with your expertise, intention, promise, target audience, and dream guest lineup.

Then we'll see you on TV!

The Biggest Questions and Doubts About Podcasts and Books

After guiding people to write hundreds of books and create tens of thousands of podcasts, here are the biggest questions and doubts that we keep coming across.

1. **"How do I know that my podcast (or book) will be successful?"**

   - First, make sure to define what success means strategically. Because if you don't know that, you can't break it down into goals, steps, and tasks.
   - Second, remember that nothing is 100 percent guaranteed. But you can get to 96-ish percent guaranteed if you have conversations with your ideal client/audience about the book (or podcast or TV talk show) that you're creating.
   - Third, keep following the Influencers Formula™ Roadmap. We've proven it. That's how we created a global radio show, podcast, two-day live event, and book—all in eight months.

   Yes it's totally doable. And it's totally okay if it takes longer. Do what supports your business and your life.

2. "I keep getting started, but then I stop, and it's still not done yet. What can I do?"

Since you've learned a lot about what doesn't work, focus on what does work instead, like:

- Having conversations about the podcast or book (always and forever)
- Using a roadmap/blueprint (which frees up your mind since you're not trying to also figure out the logistics)
- Following a timeline (with calm, patient, and persistent action)
- Accountability and community
- Giving yourself permission and forgiveness
- Smiling, relaxing, breathing, and continuing to smile

And don't forget dictation because it captures your authentic voice. You can speak 1,200 words in seven minutes (because you're an expert). Seven minutes (or 1,200 words) is 5 percent of a 25,000-word book!

3. "But I just don't have the time to write my book (or record my podcast)."

Good news! Time is no longer a barrier.

When you're having conversations with ideal clients, you know what content to include. It only takes one financial quarter to get it done. With a roadmap or blueprint, you know exactly what goes where. And when to do it.

4. "How do I work with a publisher and an editor?"

There are a million and one answers to this question, and it's a bit like the Wild West out there. So the most important things are to:

- Find a publisher who does professional self-publishing versus traditional publishing. This way, you own your intellectual property, and you're in complete control.
- Make sure they do everything (editing, cover, interior, distribution, keywords, categories, etc.).
- Understand their workflow, timeline, and expectations.
- Read testimonials and see if you can speak to one of the current or former clients of the publisher.

5. "Is it really worth it?"

Let us ask you this first. How much is one new client worth? Or one keynote? Or one consulting gig?

- If (thanks to your podcast or book) you attract one extra new client each month, would that be worth it?
- If you put your book in the hands of 100 of your ideal clients, and 10 percent of them choose your high-ticket offer, would that be worth it?
- If you could have a way to amplify your message (that people love and carry with them on their phones), would that be worth it?
- If you could create a legacy for the future and a living legacy for today, would that be worth it?

- If just one person chose your high-ticket offer, would that be worth it?

It's time to position yourself as a unique expert, authority, or thought leader with your podcast, book, or TV talk show.

You already impact and transform people's businesses and lives through what you offer. Are you ready to turn up the volume?

The path is simple. It's The Influencers Formula™ Roadmap.

Realize that you now have the right path and an array of strategies and approaches to make it happen.

So, remember:

1. Thanks to your book, podcast, or TV talk show, you can easily get one high-ticket client (whether that means $5,000, $50,000, or $500,000).
2. *But be careful* because it's easy to make mistakes that can easily cost you ten years and two million dollars or more.
3. Keep it simple.

Be seen.
Be heard.
Be easy to follow.
Be the solution.

Think about all the people who need what you offer and are waiting for you.

Imagine the impact you will make!

(And we're here to help whenever you're ready at www.DonnaAndBen.com.)

Wrapping it All Up

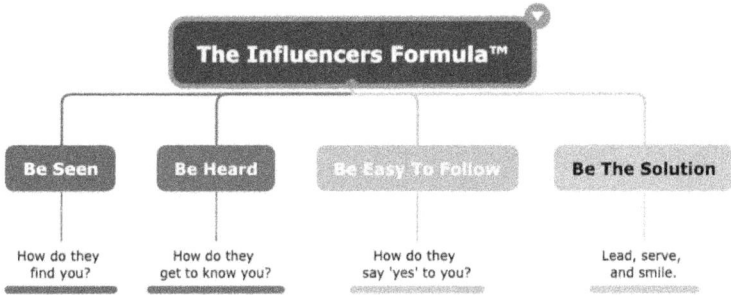

The Influencers Formula™

Be Seen	Be Heard	Be Easy To Follow	Be The Solution
How do they find you?	How do they get to know you?	How do they say 'yes' to you?	Lead, serve, and smile.

T hanks for reading. All of a sudden, we're at the end of the book. Thanks for taking the ride!

- We promised that if you've read (or listened to) this book, you will know how to make an impact as a highly paid expert authority or thought leader with your podcast, book, or TV talk show.
- We debunked the biggest myths, mistakes, and misperceptions about podcasts and books. You've also discovered how to avoid the bad decisions that cost people a dozen years and a couple of million dollars (at least).
- You now know how easy it is to create a global, thought leadership masterpiece so you can amplify your message and elevate your business.
- The doors are open for you to focus on attracting revenue and partners right out of the gate (ROI right now).
- You've explored making yes easy, referral triggers, and the many voices of story. Plus, what you need to know about meditation, imagination, and the power of your subconscious for bringing your message to the world.
- Your eyes were opened to an unexpected combination of false beliefs, forgiveness, and leadership lessons from Nelson Mandela.
- You learned the keys for business podcasting made easy, writing your book faster than the average bear, and how to skip paying your publisher an extra $180,000. You also discovered the million-dollar timeline, how to choose your best stories, and how to make sure your podcast (or book) will work.

You now know how to do your podcast, book, or TV talk show the right way. Because making the choices that bring high-ticket clients and profitable opportunities is infinitely better than losing a dozen years and a few million dollars (at least).

It all starts (as does everything in business) with knowing your audience. From there, you can do things like leverage your content and collapse time.

This book is an ongoing invitation. To choose the simplest ways to get the right things done in your business so you can live more of your life.

You now have the keys to reach more people with your message. Podcasts and books bring leads, clients, partners, and opportunities. Every successful leader, consultant, coach, solopreneur, speaker, entrepreneur, and small business owner has a podcast or book that works.

So let's get it done, shall we?

Visit us at www.DonnaAndBen.com today!

Acknowledgments

[DONNA] Writing this book has been a remarkable journey, and I am deeply grateful for the incredible support and encouragement I received along the way.

To my loving family, thank you for being my foundation of strength and for believing in my crazy endeavors, including this book. Mom, Lizzy, and Sam, your unwavering love and support have been my driving force.

To my dear friends, your endless listening and feedback have meant the world to me. Thank you for being incredible cheerleaders.

To my mentors and colleagues, your wisdom and guidance shaped me as a writer, coach, and business owner. Your belief in my potential pushed me to new heights.

To all who contributed to the research and interviews, thank you for sharing your knowledge and experiences, making this book a more valuable resource.

To the countless others whose support may not be mentioned, your encouragement and kindness are deeply appreciated.

To our readers, your curiosity and openness to new ideas inspire me to continue sharing my thoughts with the world.

This book stands as a testament to the power of support and camaraderie. To my family, friends, colleagues, and mentors, like Ben Gioia and William Eastman, your presence made this journey possible. Thank you all for being part of this adventure.

[BEN] Big thanks and a shout out to Donna Kunde for sharing this writing journey (my fourth book). So much love and thanks to my family, friends, and the animals who I've had the privilege to know and love. To my dear friend, George Schofield, who invited me to life as an entrepreneur. To Eben Pagan for the foundations. And to Bhante Vimalaramsi for sharing the teachings of the Buddha—the ones that truly end suffering—and making awakening available, in this lifetime, for almost everyone.

www.ingramcontent.com/pod-product-compliance
Lightning Source LLC
Chambersburg PA
CBHW020205200326
41521CB00005BA/252